I'VE NEVER BEEN HERE BEFORE

Ashley Campbell

TEN PEAKS PRESS®
EUGENE, OR

The quote of 1 Thessalonians 5:16-18 is taken from the *Holy Bible*, New Living Translation, copyright © 1996, 2004, 2015 by Tyndale House Foundation. Used with permission of Tyndale House Publishers, Inc., Carol Stream, Illinois 60188. All rights reserved.

Cover design by Faceout Studio, Jeff Miller
Interior design by Faceout Studio, Paul Nielsen
Photography by Ashley Campbell and Corbett Campbell
Olive branch illustration by Faceout Studio, Amanda Kruetzer
Interior illustrations by Lesley Zellers and Ashley Campbell
Photo on page 272 and family photo on back cover by Elisabeth Rose Photography

Ten Peaks Press is a federally registered trademark of the Hawkins Children's LLC.
Harvest House Publishers, Inc., is the exclusive licensee of this trademark.

I've Never Been Here Before

Copyright © 2025 by Ashley Campbell
Published by Ten Peaks Press, an imprint of Harvest House Publishers
Eugene, Oregon 97408
www.harvesthousepublishers.com

ISBN 978-0-7369-9105-6 (hardcover)
ISBN 978-0-7369-9106-3 (eBook)

Library of Congress Control Number: 2024950111

Printed in Columbia

25 26 27 28 29 30 31 32 33 / NI / 10 9 8 7 6 5 4 3 2 1

To Chris, Corbett, Hudson, Everett, Breese, and Evann.

Anywhere with you is my favorite.

CONTENTS

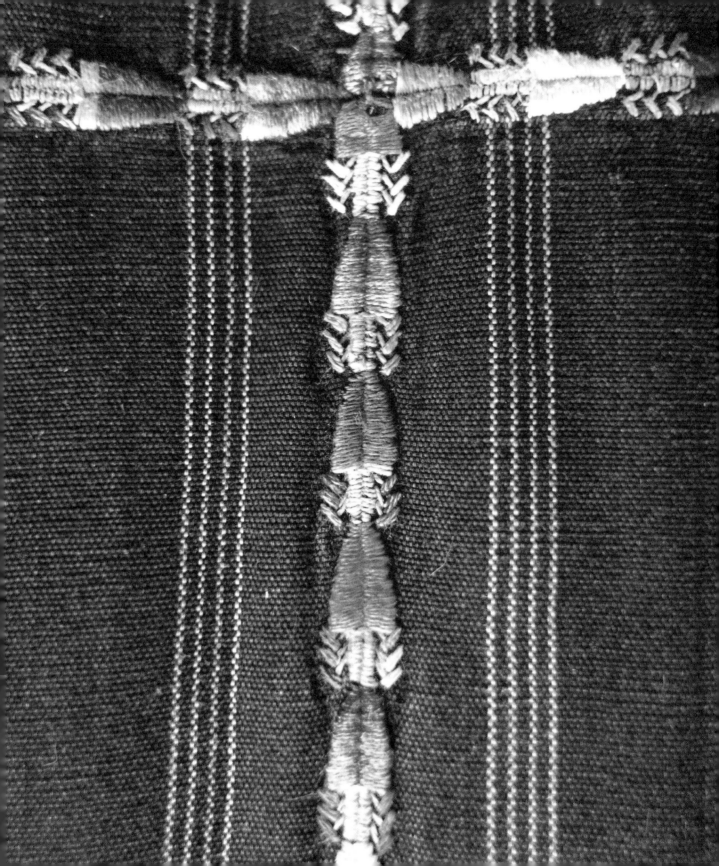

THE DREAM

Corbett grinned, snapping his helmet and turning the moped key. As a toddler, he was my only runner. I chased him across countless playgrounds and church hallways while he laughed, relishing his chance for independence. The older he got, the less I chased and the more I cheered. He was eighteen now, and after six months of traveling around the world with his parents and four siblings, he needed time for a solo adventure.

It was Thanksgiving Day, and the streets were damp from the daily Indonesian rain. I wasn't sure a moped on island hills was the best decision, but the thrill of exploring alone was one I profoundly understood. My acceptance that my days are numbered sparks my desire to live a full life rather than white-knuckling along in fear trying to ensure I live a long one.

Corbett made it back to our hostel in one piece. I could see in his eyes that his soul had been fed by an evening in which he felt wildly alive. It was a dream come true for us both.

Born to Wander

Growing up, I didn't travel internationally, but my parents routinely encouraged my sister and me to try stuff. If we needed help, tools, or support, they were available. They instilled in me a belief that most things

can be figured out, and the first step was to go for it. For sixth-grade English class, I wrote a short-story assignment about how the same sun rises and sets for all of us regardless of our location on the planet—a strange topic for a preteen girl raised in the same small town her parents grew up in. It was also a heads-up for my parents that their daughter imagined life far beyond our town, our country.

I would spend road trips gazing out the window at Oklahoma hills while daydreaming about what it would be like to sit under an acacia tree in Kenya with the Turkana or dive into the Philippine Sea with those who called the islands home. My wanderlust for distant lands was fierce, which is why in high school I loved listening to my friend Chris recount stories of trips to a little Mexican village with his family or talk about exchange students who spent weeks at his house. His love of people and diversity and his fearlessness of the unknown fueled my interest in travel (and him) all the more. I wanted to explore the world in a gritty, learn-from-people way, and I could tell Chris wanted the same.

After high school, we headed to the same college and began dating. I spent that first summer in Alaska while he backpacked through Southeast Asia. By our sophomore year, my parents came to terms with my longing to travel outside the United States. Their friends' college-aged kids wanted to spend summer break in Cancun, while I had a far different destination in mind. I boarded a plane for Asia, where Chris and I taught English in Kazakhstan for eight weeks.

One free weekend, we took a random local train and jumped off at the first stop (this is probably precisely why my parents didn't want me traveling internationally). Things could have gone wrong, but they equally could have gone right. And they did. There were no cell phones with Google Maps, and Wi-Fi wouldn't be common for another five years. We couldn't go to online strangers for guidance; instead, we overcame language barriers and asked real-life strangers for help.

I don't remember where we went on that train ride or how we returned. But I do remember experiencing the kindness of locals and eating the best soup of my life at a tiny table in a completely unknown place.

Twenty years later I would taste the only soup that would rival it—at a sticky table on a food street in Chiang Mai, Thailand, surrounded by my five kids and Chris. When I close my eyes, I remember exactly how I felt in both places. I'll never know if the Kazakh soup was that good or if it was that I had found someone who embraced the unknown with gusto and a "We'll figure it out" philosophy too. I'm guessing it was both.

A Future Hope

After Chris and I graduated from college and got married, we heard the cliché warning to have all our fun before settling down, especially regarding international travel. It's the equivalent to parents of toddlers being told, "Enjoy it now because one day they'll be teenagers." Doom and gloom. No, thanks. (Teenagers are fantastic, by the way.) We like figuring out stuff for ourselves—we didn't listen to either narrative. We knew somehow we could combine our love for international cultures with our desire to raise a family.

Our first jobs out of college landed us in Hawaii helping international students acclimate to a new country and university life. Then our next adventure was due in nine months. Before we knew it, Corbett was a toddler, and I was sitting on the kitchen floor reading an article about a family of four that traveled the world for a year. The interview awakened a dream in me. When Chris arrived home from work, I shared the article, and we agreed we should do that one day.

Fast-forward. Our family of three turned into a party of seven with the arrivals of Hudson, Everett, Breese, and Evann. Our dream grew alongside our kids and became a lens through which we made nearly every decision. For seventeen-ish years we savored each season. Our roots continued growing deeper into the Oklahoma soil, but in the background, hopes for adventure in faraway places steadily hummed.

In between managing daily responsibilities and decisions, Chris and I would talk with great excitement about how we couldn't wait for our kids to experience the high of being in the unknown and the thrill of feeling fiercely awake to life in a new place. We dreamed of coming alongside them to help them understand different cultures, religions, struggles, and lives so that they might become people of compassion, empathy, and understanding. We wanted them to recognize false narratives and stereotypes when they heard them and not to fear what doesn't align with their beliefs, opinions, or views. And we wanted to give them a fuller view of the wonder of God's infinite imagination expressed through the people and places he created.

I think the best international travel involves observing and experiencing people and places like one would study an artist. If the only work I ever saw by da Vinci was the *Mona Lisa*, I would have a restricted view of his creative genius. I'd miss learning from and appreciating him as an inventor, scientist, sculptor, engineer, and architect.

When I step into a culture with people who look and think differently than I do, when I stand on a beach with sand unlike any I've felt before, when I hear songs in languages I do not speak, when I taste food with flavors I've never savored—I'm gaining glimpses into the awe-inspiring creativity of God. It leaves me aching for more. Chris and I had hundreds of reasons we wanted to take a year to travel, but at the top of the list was our desire to broaden our kids' views of both the world and its Creator.

After traveling together and with others, Chris and I recognized characteristics that make travel far more enjoyable. Things like being open to new experiences, new foods, and calculated risks. And a big one—not letting fear be the loudest voice in your head. We couldn't force these characteristics on our kids, but we worked hard to help cultivate them.

When they were preschoolers and elementary aged, we bought a twenty-five-foot 1966 travel trailer that did not have a bathroom and drove our crew around the United States exploring its beauty and diversity. Since five-star resorts were not in our budget, we knew flexibility with sleeping, eating, and imperfect facilities would be crucial if we were to enjoy the places around the world we dreamed of visiting. Those skills are hard to teach your kids if you never change things up.

We camped as often and in as many settings as possible. We carried our shower caddies to stand-alone bathrooms, stomped on spiders in the stalls, and taught bathroom tricks to serve our kids well when their feet hit the ground in an area without the conveniences they were used to. They were comfortable with the uncomfortable.

We agreed that our family was made for cross-cultural travel, and we recognized many things were working in our favor. We would not need to plan for food allergies, health conditions, medications, or neurodivergent needs. We had unique personalities, perspectives, and struggles; yet, when it came to the situations that adventure delivers—those causing worry, tension, and fear for most—we all responded with excitement, curiosity, and contentment. I couldn't explain it, but I knew it was different.

Not surprisingly, our biggest hurdle was financial.

"How will this affect our trip?" became the question we asked for big decisions like remodeling our house, and little decisions like buying half gallons of ice cream to eat at home instead of individual frozen custards from the local creamery. There were no "Budget for a Family of Seven for a Year of Global Travel" blog posts to help. We saved all we could without knowing how much it would cost. We rarely ate out. We bargain shopped. And while my Pinterest boards showcased dreamy green tile

> When I step into a culture with people who look and think differently than I do, when I stand on a beach with sand unlike any I've felt before, when I hear songs in languages I do not speak, when I taste food with flavors I've never savored—I'm gaining glimpses into the awe-inspiring creativity of God.

for my kitchen, I opted for the cheapest white tile from Lowe's, hoping that one day I'd see *riads* in Morocco covered in handmade tiles. Day by day, year by year, we put small amounts into our savings and lived constantly between the present and the future.

When Dreams Become Goals

June 2022, the month after Corbett graduated high school, became our departure date. Our kids had years to process and prepare emotionally to be gone for a year. They heard no to so many things their friends' parents were saying yes to that they basically graduated from a master class on delayed gratification.

Things started to fall in line. I adjusted the kids' homeschool curriculum with a year away in mind. Our cat, Poppy, died while the world was on lockdown, and our chickens moved next door, preferring our neighbor's heated coop over ours. Dear friends agreed to rent our home, and my father-in-law offered to keep our dog. Suddenly, Chris was working out the details of transitioning his job to a remote position, and I was sending off applications to update our passports.

Even as the way was becoming clear, I still feared the personal devastation I'd feel if the trip didn't happen. Instead of saying, "When we leave..." I opted for "If we leave..." as a subtle attempt to protect my heart. To keep moving toward the hope of the dream becoming reality, I booked places to stay in countries like Slovenia and Albania. I researched bus stops and trains and figured out the cheapest way to get from point A to B...whatever A and B were. I multiplied every cost by seven and sleuthed ways to create an epic adventure on a budget. I made it up as I went, leaning into what felt natural and right to me.

While driving between basketball practices and play rehearsals, I daydreamed about late-night conversations on the rooftops of hostels. I couldn't wait to laugh with my kids at all the things that would go wrong and shake our heads in wonder at all the things that would go right. I was giddy with anticipation of seeing the world through their eyes and of them watching me without the burdens that I typically carry. At home, I constantly wrestle with my role in changing the not-so-good I notice in my own community. When I travel, I am quick to notice and celebrate the lovely as a short-term guest. I exhale.

Before we knew it, we were celebrating Corbett's graduation one day and packing up the house the next. We sold our cars to have additional funds and to avoid paying for insurance while gone. Our friends threw us a huge going-away party, at which sixteen-year-old Hudson (always one to bring the fun level up several notches) let his friends shave his head. We hugged. We said our goodbyes. We went to bed living one kind of life and woke up to begin a new one.

A Plot Twist on the Way to Adventure

The plane door closed.

My heart pounded with adrenaline. I had double-checked my fanny pack for seven passports as we walked through the airport's revolving door. Seven carry-on-size backpacks and decades of dreaming were all we'd take with us.

I had imagined this moment through years of steady sacrifices and careful planning, and now it was real. The tears fell as I thought, *We're off. We're actually doing this!*

We landed in Miami, and as we hurried to board our plane to Morocco, the flight crew announced a weather delay. After hours of waiting, they canceled and told us all other flights to Morocco that week were sold out. We reminded the kids that much of our trip would involve plot twists and pivoting—and those twists just kept coming.

The airline promised us hotel rooms and dinner vouchers...but there were no rooms and the restaurant had closed for the night. While Chris helped international travelers at the check-in desk, the kids and I made beds out of lounge chairs by the pool and ate selections from the snack bar. I was no longer parenting young kids but, instead, traveling with independent and flexible teenagers who saw the adventure and humor of our situation too. I rarely get overly excited, stressed, or worried. This trait could be considered boring, but it is my superpower when traveling. There are a million worse ways to spend a night than eating a Snickers by a pool with my favorite people in lounge chairs next to me.

We would experience another two days of plane delays. One round after being on the tarmac for hours before being deboarded due to stormy weather. The tension from angry passengers was as heavy as the Miami humidity. Fatigue and hunger, two traits that can bring out the ugly in all of us, marked every traveler. The kids and I talked about the situation, reflected on the good we witnessed, and discussed how to be on that side of the story by recognizing ways to defuse high-pressure situations.

Dinner that night was supposed to be *tagine* on a Marrakech rooftop, not pizza delivery in Florida. But there was beauty here too. I enjoyed time with the kids, and Chris was once again helping international travelers navigate a complex situation. We were keenly aware that soon, instead of being the helpers in our country, we'd be the ones helped in countries far away.

The Miami sun welcomed us to a new day, another booking issue, and another delay. I began looking for hidden cameras behind airport plants in case we were unwittingly starring in a reality show of travel mishaps. Thankfully, our booking was corrected, the flight took off, and we landed in New York in time to board the final leg to Morocco. As I gazed out the window at the skyline disappearing below the clouds, I felt an overwhelming sense of peace with whatever the coming year held.

We knew multiple flight delays hadn't delayed our adventure, because hiccups and plot twists are what enliven the journey. I smiled and closed my eyes, whispering, "And we're off."

This time, we really were.

While I included the names of large cities throughout the following chapters, I intentionally chose not to name the smaller towns. The beauty we experienced as we wandered the globe resulted from our approach to travel, not in following a guidebook or checking off a list of "must-see" destinations. Small towns dot the world's countryside, extending invitations to slow down and savor community. Take the detour to the unassuming, linger in the park, wander into the tiny bakery, and discover the beauty that isn't on a travel list.

MOROCCO

A donkey pulling a cart with a man questionably balanced on a little metal seat passed me as we entered the Marrakech Medina. The sight made me ridiculously happy. Weathered by time, square stones paved the single-lane path. Leather bags hung outside a small shop beside carved wooden doors with hand-painted tiles for sale. Various tarps and fabrics stretched overhead. Pale-pink clay walls made it clear why the town is known as Morocco's Red City. The fragrance of North African spices and roasting meat wafted through the dry air. I could feel the sweat soaking the parts of my shirt hidden by my backpack and expected Indiana Jones to fly around a corner at any moment. I dodged a tiny moped as I jogged to catch up to my family. "This place is amazing!" said twelve-year-old Breese, hungry and sweating but also grinning. I couldn't agree more.

The oldest section of the city of Marrakech is known as the Medina. Surrounded by ramparts, it dates to the twelfth century. Within its walls, travel is by foot, speeding carts, donkeys, and mopeds. Cars are not allowed. We wandered through a labyrinth of *souks* (Arab bazaars), *riads* (traditional Moroccan homes with enclosed courtyards), and food stalls. Every building butted up next to the other, creating an endless maze. It was enchanting and exciting and instantly made us forget the days-on-end hassle of delayed flights leading up to our arrival.

Left. Right. Donkey. Moped. Right. Another right. Eventually, and impressively, using Google Street View, Chris led us through the maze of narrow paths to our first home of the trip—a *riad*-turned-hostel. We knocked on the

door and entered the courtyard, and before we could even unload our backpacks in our room, the host was pouring us cups of tea with mint sprigs. We collapsed on a floor sofa and boho cushions, piling our backpacks nearby. The black-and-white-checkered tile, brightly woven rugs, wood serving trays, and thoughtful hospitality created a dreamy setting.

Most hostels have the option to book private rooms or bunk rooms. Typically, the kitchen and gathering areas are shared by guests. There is an art to booking hostels as a family. It primarily involves reading reviews and descriptions carefully to find the best fit for needs and preferences. After savoring mint tea, we settled into a tiny bunk room with a private bathroom—three bunk beds, each mattress narrower than a twin-size bed. For the same price, I could've booked a room with more beds but with a bathroom shared by other guests. As a middle-aged mom of five with a bladder to match, I opted to share a miniature twin bed with Evann, ten, to avoid walking down the hall in the middle of the night. It was a wise decision.

We were out to explore within an hour, mainly because Breese was on the verge of a hunger-induced breakdown. With *mille-feuille* (layered pastry) goodness in my stomach, my face started aching from smiling. After all those years of waiting, wondering, and even doubting...it was real. I was walking the streets of Marrakech, Morocco, with my family. I could hear its music. I could breathe in its spices. I could taste its sweetness. I could see its colors. It was real. The dust covering my sandals proved it. Chris and I both wore enormous grins as I held out my phone for a celebratory selfie.

For dinner, we headed to Jemaa el-Fna Square—an expansive open-air marketplace in the center of the Medina. Named a World Heritage Site by UNESCO, the entire square felt like a stage celebrating Morocco's historical and modern cultures. Once a site for public executions, it now overflowed with

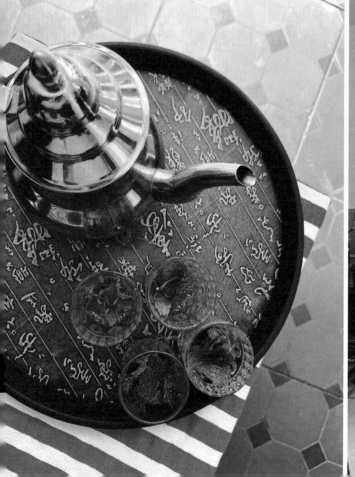

creativity—artists, musicians, performers, vendors, food stalls, tourists, and locals. Competing musicians supplied the rhythm to merchants and vendors, who yelled for attention. Cobras danced to the music of flutes. Women offered henna tattoos, while men lured tourists into paying for pictures with monkeys dressed in shiny suits. In the center of it all, things felt chaotic. From a distance, it looked like choreography and sounded like a symphony.

After stopping by a nearby ATM, we left the square for the small adjoining passages that extended in every direction. Typically, the closer a restaurant is to a tourist hot spot, the more expensive it is. Budget-friendly options are usually just a few blocks away. We filled up on *shawarma*—a ten-dollar total cost. Making our way back toward our hostel, we were inundated with yells from vendors to try the various foods and juices. Corbett shouted back that we had already eaten. One man called back with a playful smirk, "But you are so scrawny!"

As we walked by a group of teenage boys, they started grinning, nudging each other, and trying to get Breese's attention. I quickly rushed up to them, waving my water bottle and, with my best mom glare, shouting, "No! No! No!" My response took me and the local teens by surprise.

Even Chris got shout-outs. Two men called him Bruce Willis. I laughed and told him that if he was Bruce, we'd buy all the rugs, pillows, and pottery to ship home. Instead, I held my ground on my travel rule: no shopping or shipping things home. I knew that if I gave in on this, it would get out of hand with seven travelers. I've never been more thankful or annoyed by my iron willpower. Morocco was a torturous place to stick to this rule.

Ibrrahne Village— the Philosophy of Yes

It was time to say goodbye to Marrakech and head to the edge of the Sahara. Based on great reviews, I had booked a tour that would take two days of driving to reach our destination. The ten-hour drive on the first day felt surprisingly short as we made stops to learn about Morocco's Berber roots, how nomads settled to form communities, and more about the Muslim faith.

We continued our route with friendly guides, but without cell connection or much of a guess to where we were on the map. Following a few dirt roads off the highway, we pulled up to a three-story dusty rose *riad* with banana leaves stretching out of terra-cotta pots. It stood alone and seemed to pop up from the dust in the barren landscape. Ushered in, we crossed through the courtyard and outside to birdsong, hammocks, linen curtains blocking the sun, and a table brimming with mint tea and cookies. It was idyllic. My kids laughed at the difference between something I book and something that comes with a booked tour. I told them to enjoy the bougie stay while they could.

Before dinner, our host invited all his guests on a walk to view the sunset from the hill. We were the only ones to accept his offer. Our family philosophy is to say yes to invites from those who live in an area because 99 percent of the time, it ends up being fantastic. The other 1 percent usually at least results in a good story. Taking the trail overlooking the tiny community was like strolling through a market, but the food was on trees instead of tables: Almonds, walnuts, olives, pomegranates, apricots, and rosemary grew all around us. From above, we could see a river oasis with palm trees and women doing laundry in the water. Red dirt stretched endlessly to the horizon. We bumped into giggling kids excited to practice their English, and teenage girls swooning at the sight of my sons. Traveling with our kids as teens was far different from when they were toddlers. We couldn't stop smiling—people are the best part of any culture.

The night ended with a feast of *tagine*, music, drumming, and dancing. Everett, fourteen, busted out his homeschool tin whistle skills on a *lira*, a traditional

> Our family philosophy is to say yes to invites from those who live in an area because 99 percent of the time, it ends up being fantastic. The other 1 percent usually at least results in a good story.

Moroccan flute. A few hours earlier, I had no idea we were pulling into one of the most unforgettable nights of our trip. The unknown gets a reputation as something to avoid. The older I get, the more the unknown establishes itself as my favorite thing to embrace.

The next day would again be filled with the unfamiliar and the wonder that goes with experiencing a place for the first time. We were heading to the awe-inspiring dunes of Merzouga at the northwestern tip of the Sahara Desert.

Just a year earlier, I had stood in a Target with a green dress in my hand. It was airy and long and perfect for travel. The trip was still a fantasy, but I bought the dress and snapped a picture as a step toward reality. Now, here I was teetering on a sandboard on the ridge of a Moroccan dune in my green dress. With one hand, I pulled up the hem, and then I surfed down the sand. We spent an hour or so climbing up, then gliding and tumbling down. There are moments and places in life that don't feel real. I had experienced a few, and this was one. The warm sand

under my feet, the still air, the silence, and the vast orange expanse surrounding me highlighted my smallness and general sense of being wholly present to the world around me. I tried with every fiber of my being to soak it all in.

Rif Mountains—Cooking and Conversation

We value experiences and interactions with others over perceived comfort, so I thought, *Why not?* when I booked a stay at a remote countryside farm with little details of what to expect. I confess that three hours into the long bus ride, I had moments of doubt. I hoped that this choice would be okay.

Our host met us at the bus station, and we piled into his car and a taxi to make our way to his home. We walked beneath a canopy of grapevines with low-hanging fruit as we entered a lovely courtyard through a gate. Within thirty minutes, Breese and Everett were learning to make bread in the kitchen using butter from our host's cousin's cow. Friendly cats surrounded Evann.

I exhaled. "This is definitely better than okay."

The outlying location meant we spent less time exploring the area and instead savored the gift of settling in. Over the next few days, Breese spent hours learning from our host's mom how to make desserts, jams, *msemen* (fried, layered pancakes), and dinner dishes. Breese's curls were pulled back in a loose braid while she chopped vegetables next to her teacher, who was several generations older and wore a scarf covering her head. They spoke with smiles, laughter, and a lot of hand gestures.

We took a day to trek to the fields to help with an abundant chickpea harvest. Within the first thirty minutes, our hands were raw and covered with cuts. We pulled off our socks to use as gloves. It was exhausting work under the hot sun. Leading us were two widowed women who worked daily from sunup to sundown to support their families. After

a few hours, we gathered beneath the shade of an olive tree. It was not a fun morning (Hudson ended up in bed for twenty-four hours with heat exhaustion), but we were grateful to learn from a different way of life.

Later, under the grapevines at the house, we dove deeply into conversation with our hosts about government, politics, religion, parenting styles, and ourselves. The space and dialogue around that table were tremendous gifts. Our differences provided opportunities to learn from and listen to each other. The way they extended hospitality and friendship marked our family—the ease of conversation about topics often too heated back home felt like a balm to my soul.

Chefchaouen—Into the Blue

Approaching Chefchaouen, from a distance, we could see its famous blue buildings nestled in the mountains. We arrived at our accommodation and settled into our rooms for a week of getting to know this town and its people.

The adrenaline and newness of travel had worn off. Breese felt the jolting shift from a predictable routine to the unpredictable gypsy life and had to forego her typical summer attire. She and I willingly traded our shorts for long dresses and pants out of respect for the more conservative culture. Some doors open only to guests who travel more humbly and respectfully regarding culture. We experienced invitations to walk through many of those doors, and it cost us only a little comfort. That feels like a big sacrifice when you're twelve and your brothers are wearing shorts.

Evann had grown weary of my "I don't know—I've never been here before" response to her questions. Chris wrestled with working remotely across several time zones. We had yet to find a basketball court for Everett. Seeing all the posts of his friends enjoying their final summer break together was hard and led Corbett to log off social media. Our family's emotions had begun to reflect the blue of the town. Chris took the guys on a hike nearby while the girls wanted a day of nothingness. I sat on my bed alone, wondering if we had made a colossal mistake. I felt energized and alive, but my concern for my kids trumped my feelings. *Can we do this for a year? If we stay the course, will it be worth the cost? Should we go home?*

The girls and I wandered the blue maze of stone and brick buildings in search of lunch. Knowing American comfort foods such as cheeseburgers and pizza were available cushioned the blow of travel for Evann, who was the most hesitant about trying new dishes. As we ate, a fun conversation ensued regarding how young the United States is as a country compared to most and how much of what we love originated in other places.

When the guys returned, I expressed my concerns about the growing homesickness I sensed among them. But despite some sadness of missing activities at home, they still held tremendous excitement for what lay ahead. After a round of gelato against the brilliant blue backdrop of Chefchaouen, we discussed how different life would look in the coming year and agreed we all wanted to keep going.

Morocco was the best possible launching pad. We had stopped dreaming about traveling the world, and we were doing it. Once we hit the month mark, everything fell into place. We had a new way of living, new habits, new perspectives, new routines, and a newfound vagabond-style life with mint tea running through our veins.

WISDOM AND WONDER

Seeing the country as a creative wonderland, Breese and I soaked in Morocco's colors, food, architecture, people, and stunning handiwork. The four weeks were the most prolonged period we had ever spent in a country that is a Muslim state. Navigating the cultural and religious differences as women proved, at times, challenging for us. The language barrier was real, so there was much we didn't understand.

It is easy to default to right or wrong and good or bad when encountering people doing things differently. That wasn't our response. Instead, we asked questions when we could and stayed awake to our surroundings, acquiring slivers of insight through observation. We gained a context and foundation that helped us learn even more, long after our feet left the red sand.

Cultural Insights

We knew so little about the Muslim faith before we arrived, and because of the graciousness of our hosts, we gained a tremendous amount of understanding by the time we left. I will forever be grateful for how our new friends welcomed us into their homes, shared meals with us, and kindly made ways for us to learn from them.

Before my arrival, I had assumed that when the call to prayer sounded, everyone would stop what they were doing and immediately turn to pray. I had wondered what we should do when those moments arrived. Instead, we'd hear it over the clanging of the market, and business for many continued as usual. It was one of the many moments in Morocco that surprised me. I relish being surprised by a new culture.

Budget Travel: Get the Seven-Night Discount

In my initial planning, I learned many accommodations worldwide offer a discount for bookings of seven nights or more. As a result, seven nights became our default number of days for each stay. A week also gave us enough time to explore slowly and get a fuller picture of each location.

Your Adventure

What feelings arise when you think of spending an extended period of time in a culture far different from your own?

ITALY

With shorts stuffed in the very top of her backpack, Breese bolted down the Jetway and to the bathroom. After a month of long dresses and pants in the North African heat, she was ready to change and tackle Rome with bare knees. Laughing, I chased after her.

We struggled to figure out the bus and train options to our Airbnb outside the city's center, which caused a late arrival and even later dinner. Chris was grumpy and irritable. Once we found a pizzeria and ordered, he left us to hunt down a snack. When we reminisce now about "breakdowns" during our trip, we all know this was Chris's moment. The guy just needed some chips!

Restaurants in Morocco had provided two to three cups, plates, and utensils for the seven of us to share. When the waiter placed seven cups and plates on our table, we glanced at each other, initially confused and then reminded of our old normal. We devoured mouthwatering pizza around two tiny tables on a side street of a Roman suburb. Except for the delivery guys on scooters picking up orders, the roads were quiet and dark. The glow of the pizzeria was the only sign of life for several blocks.

It was a moody, memorable, and ever-so-perfect night.

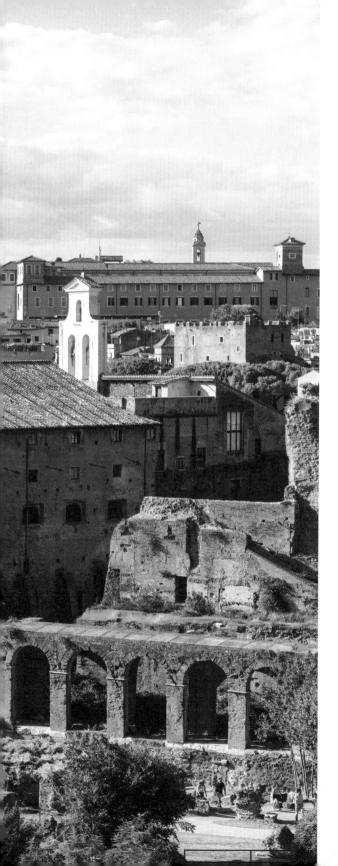

Rome—the Ancient and New

Early the next morning, we left our apartment to explore with zero expectations and abundant curiosity. Right outside our door, we discovered one of Rome's twenty-five hundred free drinking fountains (*nasoni*). Taking turns to get a drink, we chuckled at how a novelty for us was ancient normalcy for Italians. Staying on the outskirts of town meant jumping on the metro to the city's heart. Along our route, I was shocked by the amount of graffiti. Though people in the United States typically see it as destructive and unwelcome, I knew that was not the case worldwide.

I had so many questions and so much to learn. Graffiti was an insightful teacher, and being inquisitive meant we spent our time in Rome looking to understand man's desire to leave his mark on this world instead of walking around grumpy about something we didn't know how to interpret. Curiosity makes life endlessly fresh and new.

Our inaugural full day in Rome happened to be Breese's thirteenth birthday, and splurging on authentic Italian food was her ideal way to celebrate becoming a teenager. Who could blame her? We sat under an umbrella with twinkling lights and ivy overhead. Bruschetta. Lasagna. Chicken Alfredo. Breese, in her new teenage glory, savored each bite. Music wafted down the pedestrian-only street. The pale-pink walls reminded me of Marrakech.

As we wandered the cobblestone streets with gelato in hand, I gasped when we turned a corner and encountered the Pantheon, initially built in 27 BC and still used as a church. I was wonderstruck—one of my favorite ways to feel. The mantra of "When in Rome..." played on a loop in my mind as I took in everything with delight and a hunger for more. I wondered how growing up in Oklahoma impacted my perspective of ancient streets. Did Europeans walk in astonishment like I did?

We followed winding paths leading to famous locations and side alleys alike. Cafés were abundant. Public restrooms were not. My eyes widened when we turned a corner and encountered the Renaissance masterpiece *Fontana del Moro*. I stood in utter disbelief that we had stumbled upon the world-renowned fountain. One of my teenagers said, "Wow! That's a big naked butt!" As a homeschool mom, I had clearly failed to teach him an appreciation of art.

I tried to play it cool as we approached St. Peter's Basilica, but after years of studying art, it would be my first time seeing a Michelangelo work in person. I could feel my palms sweating as we walked through the massive doors. Turning to the right, there she was—the *Pieta*. A tour group walked away, leaving me alone before Mary and Jesus. She was fragile yet steady and strong. I wept. Interrupting my moment, with a smirk Everett quipped, "So you finally got to see the Petra." Considering Petra is an ancient city in Jordan, and the *Pieta* is a famed sculpture, he found his joke hilarious and I debated leaving him behind. Whichever sibling referred to Bernini's art as a big naked butt could stay back with him.

Though our "must-see places" checklist was small, the Colosseum was near the top. After reading about it and seeing pictures for decades, walking into it was wild. Names etched in stone from first-century Romans reflected the modern spray-paint tagging we noticed on our first day and reminded us of graffiti's long-standing role in the city. The excitement of being somewhere historically significant was quickly replaced by an immediate sinking feeling as we took our first glances at the arena floor. There was no escaping the brutal history of enslaved Jews having to build a structure where countless lives were sacrificed purely for the entertainment of others. And I wouldn't want to escape it. History can be painful, but I long to learn from it. It's a big reason we were there.

Not moved by art and history like their mom, my guys needed a basketball court. It had been a month since they had played. We decided not to tour a few iconic locations and instead let our sons play hours of basketball with some Italian men. After one of my sons made a good block, I heard a *"Mamma mia!"* shout directed at him. In the mental list of travel guidelines I make up as I go along, experiencing playful banter among strangers and connecting with locals is definitely worth a change of plans.

In fact, this scene of engaging with modern Rome while surrounded by ancient structures was an ideal takeaway image. This city can be chaotic and overwhelming, but the juxtaposition of old and new is exhilarating and enthralling. Typically, as one who does not like big cities, I was delighted how Rome spoke to me.

Cinque Terre— Hiking Between Villages

Catching a train from La Spezia at daybreak meant we could beat the heat and crowds hiking Cinque Terre, the five picturesque villages connected by a coastline hike. For miles, we trekked alone, passing dreamy farms and spectacular cliff overlooks. In each town, candy-colored buildings lined cliffs that rose from the water, rocks jutted up from the waves, and pink bougainvillea swayed in the breeze. It was clear why Cinque Terre had become a dream destination for travelers.

Along our way, we stopped for baked goods, lemon slushies, and detours for exploring. As Hudson climbed rocks with others and backflipped into the sea, I overheard a mom with a US accent comment it was scary to watch. She wanted her son safe and was grateful he wasn't there to see Hudson. I understand how the definition of *safe* varies person

to person, but this moment highlighted an observation I had made long before we were traveling—American culture was steeped in an obsession with perceived safety.

I wasn't nervous watching Hudson. He might be the first to jump, but he is also the first to know the water depth, look for obstructions, check rock stability, and assess all the other essential factors before leaping. I would be far more concerned if I noticed him walking past an excellent jumping rock with no desire to leap. He has never broken a bone and had stitches only once. A cracked glass pierced through a trash bag, cutting his leg when he took the trash out. I still want him to do household chores, which has proved far riskier than cliff jumping.

The afternoon approached and the scattering of people grew into a crowd. Cruise ships docked at nearby towns, and passengers flooded the trains to reach the five villages. We were grateful to be leaving as the masses arrived.

Genoa—an Unexpected Street

As we turned down the street to our apartment in Genoa, signs in numerous languages and a more somber vibe felt drastically different from anything else we had experienced in Italy. We noticed more international shops and ethnic diversity among those strolling the streets. We discovered we were staying on one of the main streets for refugees, asylum seekers, and those migrating from other countries. We dove into learning and discovery mode.

We ate Senegalese chicken for dinner and watched the movie *Rise* (an age-appropriate springboard into conversations about refugees with our youngest). We bought groceries from a Bengali store and found a Moroccan bakery whose owner was from a town we visited. We spent money at grocery stores instead of ticket booths and were anthropologists studying culture in the produce and sauce aisles. As

We spent money at grocery stores instead of ticket booths and were anthropologists studying culture in the produce and sauce aisles.

a family, we talked about what many people and families on our street were facing or had faced. We learned about the waves of migration to Genoa and their impact on the city. For several days, we got a different taste of Italy as we took in the sights, smells, stores, and languages along the diverse stretch. It was an unexpected gift.

Also unexpected, but not quite feeling like a gift, was the heat wave that had settled over Italy. With several family members deeply missing the cool breeze of air-conditioning, we took a bus to a nearby beach for respite. Sitting in the shade, I watched a small group of Italian women in their seventies splash in the water. They were, without question, having a roaring good time. Dark tans and wrinkles marked their bikini-clad bodies, not defined muscles or smooth skin. I was mesmerized by the way they enjoyed themselves and each other.

Later that night, I opened Instagram to see several posts about products and methods to look younger or lose weight. The messages came with an underlying theme that the appearance of age should be avoided and even feared. It sure seemed like the women on the beach with decades of sun-kissed wrinkles knew a thing or two that those seeking smaller waists and youthful skin were missing.

Venice—City on Water

Staying on the outskirts of tourist destinations usually resulted in substantial accommodation savings, so I booked us an apartment off the main island of Venice, about a fifteen-minute bus ride away. It was the ideal spot—local and quiet, with an Aldi grocery store and a basketball court nearby.

With two days available for exploring, we took a vaporetto to the opposite end of Venice. The ride reminded me of cruising lakes in Oklahoma on a pontoon boat—only the backdrop was a twelve-hundred-year-old city with magnificent architecture. For the remainder of the day, we slowly walked through the canals, working back to where we started. All roads in Venice lead to water. It would be difficult to get too lost.

We avoided crowds and additional expenses by foregoing the museums, restaurants, and famous tours. Instead, we watched as boats made residential and business deliveries like the Amazon trucks did at home while others transported produce and dry goods to restaurants. We were fascinated by the daily routines of a city on water. Most tourists stuck to one congested strip, jockeying for photos and standing in lines. We wandered the quiet paths, soaking in every bit of the layered beauty, rose-colored glass, and faded pastel paint.

Breese and I stood on one of the four-hundred-plus bridges looking out at the city as a gondolier passed below. I was speechless as I savored a full-circle moment. Nine months earlier, Breese had noticed

I was having a rough day. After sharing my struggles with her, I took an early shower to feel better. When I emerged from my room, she was waiting with a Reese's Peanut Butter Cup, the space heater, and the TV turned to Rick Steves's tour of Venice. She reminded me we'd be there one day. And what a sweet day it was when, months later, we shared that view together.

Sometimes, the limitations of budget and time can feel stifling or highlight what might be missed out on, but those confines often make a place less overwhelming and lead to quiet, meaningful memories. For us, dropping the typical tourist agenda created a Venice experience full of wonder and beauty.

We spent our last night on the apartment building rooftop watching a concert in a park below. As the sky grew dark and the lights of Venice twinkled in the distance, Breese and Corbett danced as a Michael Jackson impersonator took to the stage. For his final song, he began "Heal the World." Reaching the last chorus, he stood silently and let the crowd finish the lines a cappella. Their voices carried across the night sky, calling in unison to make the world a better place.

I listened to their voices and closed my eyes in agreement. This trip would be a year of rubbing shoulders around the world and being reminded how deeply good people, kind deeds, and unexpected joy overflow from every corner.

WISDOM AND WONDER

Noticing the beauty in Italy came effortlessly to me, but it didn't mean I was blind to the opposite. In Rome, we learned about the opposing views on partnership with the United States and the European Union from a protest related to the presidential election. In Genoa, we heard the complicated stories of migration. In Cinque Terre and Venice, we grappled with the effects of climate change, mass tourism, and the cruise industry on communities. Alongside the wonder we witnessed, we dove into the complex political, cultural, and religious challenges in Italy and every country we visited.

All over the world, contrast is evident. I witness some showing extreme kindness while others are rude, people picking up trash as another person tosses litter to the ground, and flowers blooming alongside weeds choking out life. I don't see the world through rose-colored Venetian glass, but I am captivated by the lovely that marks every corner.

When I walk down a new street, my eyes turn toward how the sun highlights mismatched tile, flowers cascade down concrete walls, pink paint makes the green plants pop, and older men gather for coffee and connection on little sidewalk stools. I am constantly bouncing my gaze and silently singing the chorus to "What a Wonderful World." I celebrate the good. I wrestle with the hard. I learn from both.

Cultural Insights

Near our first hostel in Morocco, a stunning painting of a veiled face covered a wall; her piercing eyes stopped me. A mural of a bare-chested woman celebrated in all her glory cloaked the ceiling of the first church I entered in Rome. The obvious differences between the two caused my mind to race with questions related to how culture, religion, and tradition impact views of the female body and women in general. Both spurred my curiosity to examine the roots of messages related to women in my culture.

Navigating differences can feel uncomfortable and awkward, but the endless surprises open my eyes to diversity of thought and practice. I'm better for it. It prompts me to observe, ask questions, and learn. Different and unexpected make for a thrilling life experience; curiosity is the easy route to get there.

Budget Travel: Be Flexible

When deciding our route from Morocco, we researched ferries and planes to multiple destinations. Surprisingly, the cheapest option was a budget airline with a destination in Rome. Since our goal was to experience the world, it didn't matter where we ended up. Flexibility with dates and destinations was the primary way we traveled as a large family on a budget.

Your Adventure

Think of a situation that makes you feel uncomfortable or awkward. What could you gain from stepping into it? What could you lose?

EVANN

age ten at the start of the trip

When I was younger, I avoided trying new things, including new foods. I was scared of the unknown. I liked knowing what I was doing and what was going to happen. I was content with my peanut butter and jelly in a bowl and yogurt. I thought, *If I like it, why change it?* That's the motto I went by for a long time. And those were the only foods I ate.

Just like it was yesterday, I remember trying something new for the first time. We went to Mazzio's every Sunday night after church to eat pizza. My parents would get me a slice of cheese pizza, cut it up, and put it on my plate. I was not going to even touch that thing. If I did touch it, it was because I was bored with watching my family eat something I didn't like, so I would amuse myself. My mom told me, "If you try a new food, I will buy you a Rubik's Cube." I wanted that Rubik's Cube, so I gave the pizza a go. On September 11, 2016, I ate pizza for the first time. I was five. My parents were ecstatic about my accomplishment. I was just waiting for my mom to buy me that Rubik's Cube. That night, we drove to Target to buy my exciting toy, which started my cubing addiction.

On the trip, I expanded my food choices. I tried things like cow brain, octopus tentacles, and caramel gelato. I hate regretting things, but I would rather regret what I did than regret what I didn't do. If I tried something, I wouldn't have to live wondering if I would've liked that food or that activity. I loved the caramel gelato.

When we had one month left, about five weeks—or thirty-six days—the trip felt like it had flown by, yet it had also gone so slowly. I had a ton of mixed feelings about the trip ending. I wanted to see my friends and family, but I also wanted to keep traveling. It made me want to cherish the moments I had with my family more. Our travels changed my life more than anyone could ever know. I would never be able to pretend the traveling didn't happen. We made memories that we would look back on and laugh about: the beach, the desert, the jungle, and the big-city life. I'd experienced all those and thought, *This world is truly amazing.* Perspective is everything; change your view and your life. When things are different, it can make us uncomfortable and scared. It's okay to be afraid but not to dislike what we don't understand.

Knowing that it's okay to be afraid let me change my perspective. I was able to try new things without being scared. Of course, it made me uncomfortable, but I did it! I had conquered my FOTNT (fear of trying new things)!

SLOVENIA AND CROATIA

As we drove east from Venice toward Slovenia, an eerie yellow smoke filled the midday sky. Hundreds of miles away, an intense heat dome had sparked the largest wildfires on record. With windows rolled up and the AC off, we inched our way along the highway, visibility clouded and sweaty legs sticking to leather seats.

An hour and a half later, the sky transformed to cobalt blue, revealing Slovenia's spectacular natural beauty. Given the limited public transportation options, we opted to rent a van, but the added cost meant our visit would be far too short. With Slovenia roughly the size of Massachusetts, we could drive about an hour and a half in any direction to explore the country. Four days wasn't ideal, but I knew we could make the most of our time before we went on to Croatia.

The DD Squad

About a year before our trip, I came across the DD Squad, a group of young adults passionate about designing and executing daring stunts. The combination of acrobatics and adventure set in epic Slovenian locations sparked my interest. After reaching out to the team, I surprised my kids on our first morning by showing up where the group practiced their latest challenge: A Rope Swing on Steroids. A crane anchored on the promenade and extended over the Gulf of Trieste launched participants a hundred feet into the air using a rope swing. Corbett shot a handful of video clips and posted them to Instagram, leading to an invitation to shoot more the next day.

Despite our limited time and the natural wonders calling to us, Chris and I wanted Corbett to take the opportunity to use his skills in a new setting. Instead of four days to explore the country, we'd be down to two. Long-term travel (and life) often calls for taking turns putting someone else's preferences over our own and learning to make the most of it.

On the second day, Hudson painstakingly watched from the sidelines. Launching that high over water came with definite risks, so it was understandable that it wasn't open to the public. But if any of my kids could step up to the swing and go for it, it would be Hudson.

As the second day of shooting wrapped up, they offered Corbett a chance to try the swing. He took a turn and asked if his brother could try, knowing how much it would mean to Hudson. I was deeply grateful for Corbett's thoughtfulness. Going for a backflip, Hudson overestimated and narrowly avoided a painful backflop. A few months later, the DD Squad posted a blooper reel from the day. It featured Hudson and his "Backflip with Extra Whip."

We missed exploring parts of Slovenia; however, Corbett and Hudson experienced an unforgettable day. I had a hunch that being slingshot from a crane in Slovenia would be among their future dad lore.

> Long-term travel (and life) often calls for taking turns putting someone else's preferences over our own and learning to make the most of it.

Ljubljana—a Farmer's Vending Machine

Within moments of stepping onto the cobblestone streets of the historical area of the capital of Slovenia, I declared it one of my all-time favorite towns. Flowers bloomed in pots, kids rode bicycles, and couples snuggled beside Venetian-inspired fountains. Soft music from street musicians with accordions and the calming twinkle of strung lights slowed life down. I savored the details of the European architecture and the most organized recycling bins I had ever seen. In every way, it was the opposite of the frenzied Jemaa el-Fna of Morocco. And yet it mesmerized me just the same.

I led my kids on a hunt for a *mlekomat*, a vending machine that dispensed raw milk. It was among the few items on my must-see list. Despite abundant dairy farms in Oklahoma, raw milk is not easily accessible due to legal restrictions.

I slid a euro in and soon held a one-liter bottle of milk. A neighboring vending machine sold fresh eggs. Both lined the perimeter of the outdoor, six-day central market. Leaning against a table, I followed a rabbit trail of thoughts regarding the differences between countries' regulations. While the United States has laws against raw milk sales, Slovenia banned school vending machines with sugary drinks. What is legal in one place can be illegal in another. I stood there fascinated by it all, and my kids poked fun at my unbridled excitement over vending machine milk.

Triglav National Park— Pretty Close to Paradise

With the kids asleep in the back of the van, Chris drove as the sun rose. Not understanding any signs and with our cell connection gone, we ended up on a toll road. Coming out of a five-mile tunnel, we were in Austria. We added it to our growing list of "oops" moments.

Back on the correct road in the right country, we logged a full day of hiking short trails in the Soča River Valley and splashing in the aquamarine water. We felt as though we had stumbled on an adventurer's paradise as we romped through the valley's otherworldly beauty. Large rocks smoothed by the current served as our picnic table as we sat downriver from a bridge dating back to Napoleon. I ached, knowing the valley and national park deserved far more time than we could spare. We were missing so much.

Driving back to our apartment, Chris spotted a few cars parked along a quiet road. Tired from a full day, the kids groaned when they realized he was making a U-turn to see what we were missing. We followed a dirt path down to the river's edge. A rustic bridge with platforms for jumping stretched across the gentle river, and a diving board made of two long pieces of wood mounted to concrete convinced

my crew it was worth the stop. Local kids splashed while adults sat nearby in foldable chairs with cold drinks in hand. Corbett jumped off the bridge, and Evann dominated the diving board. The sun's reflection on the water slowly disappeared in the no-frills local treasure.

We collapsed in the van and cruised through sleepy towns and stretches of lush green mountain valleys. Red-roofed buildings stood at attention along a quiet river as matching flowers blew in the wind. Though homes dotted the landscape and shops intermittently lined the street, we seemed all alone. It was as if the entire countryside went to sleep at nightfall. I didn't want to leave.

Basketball and Bled

While my kids preferred that I make plans and trusted me to pick locations and experiences I knew they would appreciate, they occasionally rattled off something that sparked their interests. Everett mentioned a visit to NBA player Luka Dončić's childhood court in Ljubljana. As we pulled down an unassuming road in the modern area of town, our first rain since leaving home began to fall. Not one to show extreme emotion, Everett grinned with deep satisfaction and contentment as he ran up and down the court.

We drove forty-five minutes northwest from the court to spend our remaining hours at the iconic Lake Bled. Pristine turquoise water encompassed the little lake island with a church perched on its top. The absence of motorized boats on the water protected the picturesque setting, the peaceful sounds, and the clarity of the water. Oklahoma lakes are a muddy shade of brown, which hides monster catfish that I'm convinced want to eat me. No, thank you. Growing up, I often commented I'd only swim in a lake with water as clear as a pool. Lake Bled easily met my conditions.

When I booked our time in Slovenia, I imagined hiking for hours, floating down rivers, sipping coffee in little towns, and lingering outdoors. I didn't imagine we'd spend it watching the creation of YouTube content, jumping off a rustic diving board, or accidentally detouring into another country. I'm a girl excited by trees, quiet nights, fresh dairy, organized recycling, and early mornings. Slovenia introduced itself to me briefly and captured my attention immediately. I was longing to return before I left.

Zagreb—Shared Grub

Croatia's capital, Zagreb, sits within a four-hour drive from Slovenia, Austria, Slovakia, Italy, Serbia, and Hungary. Based on years of playing the Ticket to Ride Europe board game, we were already familiar with the train routes in and out of the city, but now we could explore its actual streets.

Under draped lights and a bunting made of white granny panties, we walked along a path leading to a spectacular view of the city's sprawling terra-cotta roofs. I took a twirl under the bunting, delighted by the unexpected cuteness of it. Colorful murals depicting patterns, plants, and politics butted up to historic buildings in pastel shades.

In the last eight weeks of travel, I quickly became a die-hard fan of pedestrian-only streets, a far less common option in Oklahoma. The handiwork beneath my feet held my affection and reminded me of when craftsmanship was celebrated more than efficiency. Pedestrian paths also meant I had zero concern about stepping off a curb and into oncoming traffic while I fixed my gaze everywhere but in front of me.

Back at our hostel, I cooked our dinner in the shared kitchen. Next to me, two young backpackers combined undercooked potatoes and a can of beans on their plates. Struggling to get it down, they glanced at us with our steaming plates of fried rice and chicken. I overestimated how much to cook, leaving us with several half-eaten dishes. Their young faces looked desperate, like they could use something a mom cooked, even if strangers had half eaten it.

Though shared hostel kitchens were not my preference, I was learning to appreciate the unique experiences that came with them. I was grateful for the chance to feed a couple of adventurous guys far from home and hopeful another mom would look out for mine when they were off doing the same.

Brač Island— an Adriatic Respite

In the stillness of morning, I pulled open the double doors leading from the kitchen to the porch patio. The longtime friends renting our home for the year had connected us to their friends who lived in Croatia. Tremendously generous and hospitable, they offered us their island home. Greeted by a towering bougainvillea, my eyes slowly scanned my new view. I could see nearly the whole village from my perch. Sandwiched between the purple blooms next to me and the blue of the sea in the distance, homes and businesses made of white limestone with matching red roofs filled the hilly landscape.

This quaint island community would be the respite we didn't plan for but needed. The biggest challenges of our travels had not been language, transportation, food, or discomfort. It was the lack of freedom for my five very independent and confident kids. While I savored my time with them, they missed the freedom of coming and going on their own.

The quaint town meant Hudson started each day at the free community gym with weights. Everett discovered a basketball court next to the water, where he met a kid from Ljubljana. Sharing their love for Slovenia led to an instant connection.

Corbett often went opposite where we went, taking full advantage of much-needed space from parental input. While Chris worked, the girls were content to float in the clear Adriatic with me.

With our toes in the pebbly beach sand, Breese and I perked up to the sound of a young boy with a British accent in a hunger-induced rage to which his mother responded, "Your father went to get the pizza. Chill out and get back in the water!" Burying our heads in our towels, Breese and I avoided making eye contact with each other lest we completely break down in uncontrollable laughter. The little guy was equally charming and irate.

The exchange caught our attention because it was the first time in two months we had heard an argument in English. We understood every discontented and frustrated word. Though the scenery constantly changed, I realized my life had become tremendously quieter, and it suited me quite well.

Nightly, we strolled past a five-star hotel. Two windows with views into the baking kitchen beckoned Breese to stop for a glimpse each evening. She learned the baking schedule, and the staff grew to expect her visits. When Breese clapped excitedly over an exquisite dessert, confusion set across the baker's face, followed by sheer delight. The feeling of being seen and appreciated is universal.

One evening a baker waved to Breese and pointed to a nearby door when a dessert was mildly imperfect. Breese walked away with a grin, a chocolate mousse, and an invitation to join them inside the next night. They welcomed her back with a hairnet, a stool, and smiles of delight. We were not hotel guests or restaurant customers; both were too far out of our budget. We offered nothing, but the team of bakers gave Breese everything. Words were unnecessary between them; the Croatian bakers and the American teenager found common ground between sugar and dough.

Dinner from the Sea

We noticed flags popping up around town and learned it was a national holiday. While listening to a live band, we spotted a line forming near the water as dusk became night. The excitement was palpable. We had no idea what the line was for, but it was clear if we didn't jump in, we'd be missing out.

Several men on a fishing boat pulled out a massive stockpot and placed it inside a shopping cart at the start of the line. Suddenly, we were holding out our hands for steaming bowls of we-have-no-idea-what. We laughed, trying to guess what we were eating. Later, we'd learn it was a local specialty: Croatian risotto, a dish made with cuttlefish, calamari ink, and other ingredients. We were in the right place at the right time, with a sense of adventure leading us—a perfect travel trifecta.

Hours later, Breese and I woke up before dawn so she could FaceTime a friend and I could catch a final sunrise. I sat on the seawall, waiting for the first light to flicker on the gentle waves. A little farther down, an older man stood outside his door and stabilized himself with a cane. A woman held a coffee mug in her outdoor kitchen. The three of us were strangers on a sliver of Croatia's six thousand miles of shoreline, but we started our day together under a painting of pink reflected on the deep-blue waters.

WISDOM AND WONDER

The lack of routine and familiarity that felt challenging during our first month of travel now felt like a respite. The break created space to begin thinking about home in new ways. I sensed the clarity that came with our time away would define the years ahead. Despite the differences in countries and experiences, we noticed patterns emerging. For me, the season of rest from obligation and the slow pace of life made room for curiosity, contemplation, and new appreciation of the world around me. I found my sense of observation heightened because I couldn't understand any of the words around me. From the outside, it looked like a whirlwind of adventure. And it was. However, we were all letting out a long, slow exhale.

Cultural Insights

History of the Lake Bled area of Slovenia can be traced back to the Stone Age and includes a period of the 1800s when an institute for natural healing flourished on its shores. Guests came to treat various conditions through fresh air, sunbathing, barefoot walks in the grass, and modest meals. In only a few days, we recognized the value of nature, health, and quality of life as core threads in the tapestry of Slovenia. As we made our way through each country and culture, we kept our eyes open to the subtle and overt differences we noticed. Observation and curiosity allowed us to recognize how politics, worldview, religion, and history seamlessly and messily intertwine each place, which helped us understand its people.

Travel Tip:
Share Meal Responsibilities

I typically book accommodations with kitchens when visiting places where eating out is beyond our budget. Shopping and cooking in other countries provide endless learning opportunities. Each day, a different family member oversaw planning the menu, shopping on a budget, and making dinner. We did this at home, but doing it with unfamiliar ingredients, translating labels and measurements, and paying in changing currencies was much more challenging. Sharing meal responsibilities boosts problem-solving skills and confidence.

Your Adventure

When was the last time you felt deep contentment, and what circumstances helped you reach that point?

BOSNIA AND HERZEGOVINA

"This is not the right station," I said, leaning over to Chris as the bus pulled into the final stop in Mostar, Bosnia and Herzegovina. I had confused the city's central bus station for the line's main station. Grateful we carried only backpacks, we could pivot quickly in another less-than-ideal situation. Thankfully, two taxis cost less than a latte back home. We drove the empty streets across town to our apartment; we were tired, hungry, and done for the day. Laws regulating what could be open on Sundays meant the evening streets were a quiet welcome to our third Balkan country.

A change of plans caused us to add a night to our time in Mostar, and the original apartment I booked was unavailable, which forced us to stay in a different area for the night. It was not ideal, but we'd roll with it. I searched Google for a nearby open restaurant or grocery store and found a tiny one a few blocks away. Breese, Chris, and I walked the narrow footpath near the road, and my face dropped as we entered the store. Squeezed into the closet-sized space, I tried to figure out how to feed our family using the items on the sparse shelves. Cereal would work, but not well, without milk. Three eggs would feed Hudson, but not the seven of us. I could skip dinner and breakfast, but the rest of my crew, not so much. Occasional "hanger" had proved to be the biggest threat to our trip enjoyment. My sanity needed them to eat.

A line began forming outside. Customers walked out of a small opening next door with what appeared to be a baked good wrapped in paper. With no other options, we hopped in line. Inching into the shop, we approached a counter like a Subway. Instead of sandwich options, large pizza pans were filled with what looked like an oversized, flat cinnamon roll. We ordered two and the woman behind the counter looked puzzled at how the three of us could eat the equivalent of two large pizzas. We couldn't understand her questions, and she couldn't understand us, so she sliced them up and slid them into paper.

Back at the apartment, we dug into the meat-filled pastry. It was delicious! Our first introduction to the traditional Bosnian dish *burek* was a happy accident—as most of our food experiences tended to be. With the hunger-induced crankiness averted, we settled in for a family movie night.

Mostar—No Longer a Front Line

As we began our way down the hill and into the oldest part of town, from our elevated viewpoint I paused to take in the shape of Mostar. The town appeared nestled in the bottom of a bowl, surrounded by hilly elevations. The surrounding hillsides made the streets and homes look trapped, and I wondered how it felt during the war in the '90s when gunfire filled the sky and destroyed bridges leading out of town.

After a short walk down, we were on the outskirts of the oldest section of town and ready to eat again. We lingered in a small restaurant specializing in meats and breads. To Everett's sheer joy, the *ćevapi* he loved in Croatia was included in the fifteen-dollar family platter. I scanned the menu and smiled to see hamburgers alongside *pileći bataci*, *pomfrit*, and *kombinacija*.

With full stomachs, we slung on our backpacks and wove through town toward our next apartment. Buildings with fresh paint and covered in fabric

> **Murals depicting pain and restoration loomed over us as we made our way down quaint and lovely streets.**

untouched since the war. An abandoned building similar to a layered parking garage dominated the skyline. It was a concrete canvas peppered with holes from gunfire and covered in graffiti and art. I wondered how many of the artists were children during the war. When they painted words like "You don't have to play by the rules," were they reflecting on stories their parents told or their own lived experiences? My guys shot three-pointers and I sat on a bench in an endless stream of questions.

Before night fell, we made our way into the historical part of town. Cobblestone walking streets had become familiar to us over the last few months. It was almost hard to remember the concrete sidewalks back home. I took mental notes of everything I saw. The date *1981* painted on several walls, street poles, and planters caught my eye. Passing stalls with bracelets and bags, I wondered how often the shop owners noticed the marks of gun shelling on the surrounding businesses. After three decades, had they grown accustomed to it? Was it a painful daily reminder of loss? Or was it both? Murals depicting pain and restoration loomed over us as we made our way down quaint and lovely streets.

signs butted up to others with crumbling exteriors. A bright pink bucket painted "Make Way for Flowers" spilled over with matching hydrangeas and welcomed customers into a floral shop. The oldest section of the town catered to tourists and offered a few boutique-style accommodations. We opted to stay in a more local neighborhood for budget reasons and the experience. Halfway to our apartment, I realized the circular chunks of missing concrete on the buildings were battle scars. When I run to a shelter, it is to hide from a tornado, not a rocket. When I see a building with chunks of missing concrete, I assume it is from faulty construction, not gunfire.

With bags dropped off in our apartment—one with a washing machine (the first in our travels)—we took to the surrounding streets. To the left, we could wind our way toward the vibrant old town. To the right, we spotted a basketball court outside a school with a stunning yellow exterior. Its pointed arch windows with white trim reminded me of Morocco.

Crossing a major street, the guys took off with their ball while I planted myself on a bench. The street was a surprising mix of restored buildings, new construction, and structures seemingly

The Mostari— Should We Join Them?

We reached the bank of the breathtakingly beautiful Neretva River. With mountains surrounding it in the distance and stone Turkish buildings erupting around its banks, it was idyllic and enchanting. Its history was not. The Stari Most, a sixteenth-century Ottoman bridge considered by many to be the crowning jewel of Mostar, arched to a point over the frigid water. Two small towers flanked each side of the bridge. In 1993, relentless bombing during the conflict destroyed the bridge and ended its 427-year legacy of soaring above the river. Rebuilt in 2001–2004, the bridge returned as the focal point for evening strolls, dining, and

shopping. Chunks that had collapsed into the river were pulled onto the banks and are now used as seating for tourists like me to savor the view and consider the history of where I sat.

Excitement filled the air as divers, known as Mostari, walked among the crowd, collecting donations and stirring the anticipation of an evening jump off the eighty-five-foot bridge. Thrill-seeking tourists were welcomed to jump after attending a training course on smaller platforms and paying a fee. Rescue boats floated in the water—severe injuries and deaths had been the outcome for many jumpers. Corbett and Hudson heavily weighed the option of jumping. I held my breath, hoping they'd decide against it and wondering how I'd respond if they wanted to go for it. I've always wanted them to take calculated risks because many opportunities come with only one chance. However, it was also early in our trip, and the risk of a trip-ending injury was too great. Ultimately, the stories of broken bones and horrific injuries led them to decide against it.

Once donations were collected, we watched a young Mostari climb over the railing on the bridge and stand precariously above the current. Bystanders roared with cheers. With a confident step off, he stretched his arms out in a T, bent his knees back, and held a statue position until seconds before hitting the water—a spectacle of bravery, history, and culture. We joined the crowd erupting in claps, caught up in the wonder of it all. Hudson turned to me with a grin. "You're going to do it, right?" He knew there was a part of me that wanted to jump, but not for a crowd.

Just past the bridge, I paused. A handwoven rug in all my favorite shades of green, pink, yellow, blue, and red hung next to silver necklaces dangling on a black cloth attached to the wall. Below them a pedestal brimmed with trinkets and a little purse with a picture of Saint Mary. A gas mask and a camo soldier's hat rested on the smooth stone ground. Everything in me wanted to buy the rug. I refused even to ask the price. Instead, I snapped a quick photo with my phone. The juxtaposition of the carpet's artistry next to the war relics reflected the opposing messages and feelings in the colorful murals we'd seen.

Growing up, I spent most Saturday nights at my grandparents' house eating takeout from Jim's Coney Island—a coney with extra relish and a slice of baklava as a special treat. I passed on my appreciation for the layered pastry to Breese, who was on a mission to find the best baklava during our travels. Like a ship directed by a lighthouse, the glow of a baklava shop called out to her. More likely to spend money on treats than I, Chris escorted her inside, and they returned with an entire sampler box. Jim's only served pecan baklava. I had no idea the dessert came in countless variations. The late-night treat served up a sweet ending to a full day—and a confirmation to Breese to always ask Chris first when it came to treats.

The Invisible Line

The complicated history of the country and the city of Mostar was challenging to piece together. I remembered learning where Yugoslavia was on a map as a child and then hearing several other countries replaced it as a teenager. No one explained the change, leaving me confused about this land.

Along with about thirty others and a local guide, we met up early in the morning for a tour of the city. For nearly three hours, we walked the streets, taking in the perplexing pieces of its story and helping the puzzle make more sense. We better understood the complexities of its history, culture, beauty, and current challenges. Mostar was home to three main ethnic groups: Roman Catholic Croats, Eastern Orthodox Serbs, and Bosniaks (Bosnian Muslims). The three groups had lived peacefully and in community before the war.

The conflict in the early '90s eventually pitted neighbor against neighbor and even family against family. Our guide explained the ethnic and religious crossroads in a way that I could understand; yet I also recognized how much more there was to learn. He pointed out common misinformation about Mostar and included personal information as one whose family had been there for generations.

He turned to my sons and said, "Teenage boys in Mostar are very jealous of you. Do you know why?" We guessed that maybe it was because we were traveling. He went on to share how that main road we had been casually crossing from our apartment to the basketball court was the front line of the war. Though the war was over, the street was a cultural divide. Many in the community will never cross the invisible ethnic line...many local teenage boys would love the freedom to travel carefree in their town the ways my guys did.

He pointed to the tall, abandoned building we had explored the day before. "That was the sniper tower on the front line." An abandoned bank building had provided a home in the sky for snipers with guns pointed toward the road that we now freely walked for haircuts, basketball, and a Marvel movie at the mall.

Before the tour ended, we stopped by a small cemetery with grave markers crammed together. Once a park where couples strolled on dates and friends gathered for fun, it had become a burial ground. During the war, Muslim residents were forced to bury their loved ones in the park under the cover of night. The haunting stories of the war and the image of the park-turned-cemetery stayed with me. I haven't looked at another cemetery since without thinking about the one in Mostar.

Out the Kitchen Window

After months of travel, I had grown accustomed to making coffee in ever-changing kitchens. However, as I went about the morning ritual, it felt very different in Mostar. The wind blew the vines on a building marred by bullet holes outside the kitchen window, and I could hear the sounds of the Muslim call to prayer and, later, church bells ringing. The melodies reminded me I was in a town marked by many cultures and beliefs. When I leaned my head out the window, I could see the sniper tower. It had been thirty years since the sounds of shelling rang outside, but as a first-time guest, I could still feel the heaviness of loss as I imagined what took place where I now stood peacefully making a cup of coffee as my family comfortably slept.

From my window, I also saw children playing, shops booming, and people going about life. There was the little restaurant where we ate plates of *ćevapi*. The *1981* painted throughout the town was a reference to the founding of a soccer team. A statue of Bruce Lee stood in the park—local love for Lee being a unifier among the division. Minarets and steeples soared in front of a blue sky. Red Coca-Cola awnings covered outdoor café seating, and older men sold jars of honey on foldout tables. A pale-pink wall read "All gave some, some gave all." When I watch the news headlines fill with stories of war, division, and destruction, I think of Mostar. Like a mural painted on a war-torn building and a colorful rug next to a gas mask, hope and beauty have figured out how to grow amid the destruction of war.

WISDOM AND WONDER

In the planning stage of our trip, several friends asked if it was safe to travel to Bosnia and Herzegovina. I'd respond with a gentle reminder that the war ended in 1995. I was the age of my kids during the Bosnian War. Sometimes, we can lose sight of time in the quick passing of our days. It can be tempting to freeze a person or place in a moment or period and believe what was once true is always true. When a handful of years passed between seeing the child of one of my friends, I was shocked by how much growth took place. A tremendous amount of change can happen in three years. In three decades, a place can become unrecognizable.

While we explored Mostar, it was impossible for me not to think of the war in Ukraine and fast-forward to my kids visiting there one day. In thirty years, they could be walking the streets of Mariupol, led by a guide and learning about the conflict that scarred its buildings and streets. Would tourists sway to music softly playing in Kyiv's streets like they now do in Mostar?

Cultural Insights

Completed in 1902, the stunning yellow school with the basketball court we frequented daily was heavily damaged during the war and later rebuilt. Our guide shared it was the only school in Mostar that integrated students from local ethnic groups. While some subjects taught to the students were the same, other subjects, such as history and language, were taught differently depending on the ethnicity of the class.

As I listened to our guide, I thought of the battles over curriculum in my state. Whether in Mostar or the United States, it was easy to see the effects and division caused by differences in how history is interpreted and taught. For all the ways the world is diverse, its similarities are also overwhelmingly apparent.

Budget Travel:
Take a Free Walking Tour

Many cities around the world offer free walking tours for visitors. Tour guides welcome donations and provide valuable insight into the history and culture of a city. For a budget traveler, free walking tours are a treasure. Larger cities often have several options in numerous languages and on various topics. A quick internet search for "Free Walking Tour _____" should pull up options. Always read the reviews before joining a tour!

Your Adventure

If you've never lived in a city under siege, what steps can you take to better understand what life is like for those who have?

ALBANIA

After intentionally arriving early to get bus seats, we settled in for the drive from Montenegro to Albania. The rows began filling, and not everyone would fit. My thoughts of gratitude for our seats were interrupted when the driver pointed to our family and then to a nearby van. Moving our family freed up a chunk of seats. By default, our shoestring budget meant embracing the unpredictability and confusion of public transportation, so we had learned to go with it. Whatever "it" was. Enjoyable cross-cultural travel also required relying on strangers and believing in the goodness of people, which typically worked for us. When it didn't, the challenge was short-lived.

Our driver hopped out at the border, leaving us and the van idling. Everett jokingly offered to drive, but soon the driver motioned us to walk toward the checkpoint. Waving to a man on the other side, we assumed we were changing vans as we changed countries. *Just roll with it*, I thought as we walked past all the cars lined up to cross the border. With new passport stamps, Chris and I shrugged our shoulders, made "well, here we go" faces, and loaded a nondescript van with our kids in a new country. Albania was already turning out to be an unforgettable adventure.

Gregarious and with a big laugh, our new driver made the best first impression of Albania. Chris sat up front, and they laughed in their attempts to communicate. After an hour of driving through wide open spaces, he dropped us off at our hostel.

Shkodër—Satellite-Sized Pizza and Hostel Hangs

The hostel was a two-hour drive from the mountains, where I had planned an epic hike from one remote mountain village to another. The staff helped us arrange transportation to the hike and store our bags for a few days, so we only had to take small daypacks. We spent a few days in Shkodër eating fifty-cent gelato and devouring pizza the size of a small satellite dish. We explored nearby castles, stumbled on concerts, and rode bikes along the river. The low-key, not-too-big city feel reminded us of home.

We took advantage of nights at the hostel to gain travel tips for other Albanian locations from fellow guests. Corbett, Hudson, and Chris joined in on late-night karaoke and gulped ice-cold water that flowed from a beer tap. Hudson declared it the best water he had ever drunk, most likely because for many months cold water had been hard to find. Peppered with questions from young fellow travelers, we ineffectively tried to explain why an eighteen-year-old in the United States cannot buy a wine cooler but can vote, serve on a jury, and purchase a gun. We welcomed every chance to hear the perspectives of others on US laws and customs they found confusing. Travel not only broadened our perspective of other

countries but also gave us the chance to glimpse our homeland through the viewpoints of others.

On our last morning, a large van with about twelve others picked us up, and we headed to the mountain village of Theth. Seeing the faces of twenty-something backpackers when we rolled up as a family seven deep was always funny. It is usually a mix of confusion and fear. I hoped we left them inspired to see travel as something they could do in their middle years and to realize that having kids did not mean the end of adventure.

Our first week in Albania included an introduction to the history. Many we met grew up under the rule of dictator Enver Hoxha, a paranoid leader with an iron grip on the country. During his reign, he oversaw the construction of over 170,000 concrete dome bunkers nationwide. The bunkers marked the Albanian landscape like tornado sirens on street corners in Oklahoma.

Residents compared Albania's isolation during communism to that of North Korea. They told stories about coming out of that period to discover events like man traveling to the moon. For many, the extreme isolation removed them from Elvis, Coca-Cola, chocolate, chewing gum, and fruit like bananas. We toured churches and mosques under construction in what was once the world's first atheist state and smiled as residents celebrated being the birthplace of Mother Teresa. The Albania they described thirty-plus years ago was vastly different from the vibrant one we were experiencing.

Theth—a Mountain Guesthouse

As my crew started a volleyball game with local kids in the guesthouse yard, I swayed in a hammock. I

> Travel not only broadened our perspective of other countries but also gave us the chance to glimpse our country through the viewpoints of others.

adored the way my kids jumped into any social situation. One little boy kept saying, "Oh, %#@$!" every time he missed the ball. I assumed he picked up his English phrases from backpackers but later learned video games contributed to his repertoire.

As the game continued, a great-grandma with dyed dark hair chased a cow down a ravine with a walking stick. Her family had lived in this lush valley for four hundred to five hundred years. I struggled to wrap my mind around a history like that in one place. I booked three nights at her family's guesthouse to learn more about her home and relax before our hike. In 1991, as an adult, she saw communism fall. Her grandson told us the family tried to get her to slow down, but after decades under extreme communism, no one could tell her what to do anymore. I longed for the language skills to talk to her but settled for attempting to get a smile. I was unsuccessful, though she freely smiled at my guys.

She interrupted the volleyball game to yell at the little guy who liked cuss words. He argued back and turned to Hudson with a mocking smile, clearly not caring what the woman said. I counted it an honor to spend a few days with this family. Knowing bits and pieces of their history and all that the Albanian people endured influenced my perspective. I might have wanted to wrap up the great-grandma in my arms if I were a hugger. But I'm not. And I imagine that would have been awkward for both of us.

Sitting on the cold bathroom floor under the guesthouse's hundred-year-old staircase, I heard footsteps going up and down above me. I didn't know if I had food poisoning, ate too many plums from the tree over the hammock, or had a stomach bug. Regardless, whatever was inside me wanted out. When I no longer heard steps, I opened the door to sneak back into my room. A perk of staying at a shared guesthouse was meeting other travelers and host families. The downsides included shared bathrooms and limited private space.

Whatever hit me soon hit Chris and two of our kids. Corbett took charge. At eighteen, he had been to eight other countries and could handle any hurdle—the most significant being feeding his siblings in a remote location. He made the trek down the forested valley, across a river, and a quarter of a mile along a dusty road to get pizza while his parents bounced between sleep and a bathroom. Just as I began to feel better, I looked outside to see him climbing up the dirt path, arms full of four pizzas. No longer a young boy, he was a man his parents could depend on, and in that moment, he was my hero.

Albanian Alps—Hiking Between Villages

The morning of our hike came fast; I was already feeling faint when we reached the trailhead. *There is no way I can do this*, I told myself. However, we had nowhere to spend the night. Our next guesthouse was over the ridgeline; there were no vacancies for seven in Theth and no transportation options. Hiking felt impossible but less impossible than getting us back to our backpacks in Shkodër. I passed my small backpack to Hudson and began climbing the mountain.

Our kids never complained as they dealt with two parents moving painfully slow and holding them back. Everett survived on gummy bears he had packed away. Hudson ran ahead and would wait, then repeat the process. A few hours in, we collapsed onto benches at a little café perched on the side of the mountain (how did they build it there?!). We will never forget those french fries, the cold Sprite, or the view—a surprise reprieve on the edge of a ridge.

Hours later, we reached the summit. Before leaving home, I regularly played "Song of Ascent" by Hillsong and pictured the day we'd reach the top of the Theth-Valbonë hike. I often doubted the trip would happen, but if we did actually make it to Albania, I promised myself I'd play the song on the summit. The climactic moment I envisioned wasn't what I expected. The view was spectacular, and I played the song, but feeling weak all day clouded the moment. Instead of dancing on the peak, I had only survived the climb.

The descent was far less challenging but still slow moving. Eight and a half hours after we left the guesthouse in Theth, we collapsed in Valbonë's soft valley grass. I had built up the glory of the mountaintop and lost track of the valley's splendor. One reminded me I could do hard things, see how far I'd come, and look to the future, but the other was where things grew and life thrived. I'm thankful for my mountaintop moments and equally grateful for the life forged and nurtured among others in the valley.

Around our guesthouse's little picnic table, we feasted on cucumbers, fried potatoes, bread, fresh tomatoes, chicken, lettuce, and cheese. After all the years of hiking with little ones and offering snack breaks every few minutes to help them reach the end, the tables had turned. Our kids carried the bags and the family morale and ensured their parents made it to the end. They were just as hungry and exhausted as their parents, but they handled the challenge with grit. I was ridiculously proud of them.

Bus Chronicles

We journeyed down the coast and landed in a bus with a spunky woman assisting the driver. The bus stopped to pick up a mom and her two young daughters walking along the route. I watched as they didn't pay and stood in the aisle with no empty seats. Following the lead of others, Evann squeezed onto Chris's lap to make more room. Suddenly, the assistant closed the curtains, and the mom and her girls ducked into the aisle. I looked out the window to see police officers. No one else seemed to notice or care. A couple of blocks later, the assistant opened the curtains, those crouching stood up, and they hopped off the bus.

We repeated the process several more times, and I could barely believe our fortune as a family. For a brief time, we were part of a team giving moms and kids free rides so they didn't have to walk in the heat.

Hiding from the police made me question the legality of it, but the heart was clear. I was in awe of how passengers willingly gave up their paid seats and comfort for the sake of others. It was fiercely beautiful and left me wondering how the decades of Hoxha's rule impacted the actions of our fellow passengers.

Soon, the assistant opened the door and motioned for our family to hop out. We were far from our destination, but she knew where we were headed, so we trusted her. However, sitting on the side of the road, confused, we wondered if we were supposed to stay put or walk somewhere. It was only a short time before a bus pulled up with the name of our next destination on the window. We climbed on board and began flying down the road.

Along the jagged coast, the driver stopped, jumped out of the bus, and grabbed a beer from a tiny shop. He chugged it. *Is anyone else seeing this?* I thought, looking around. Everett was vibing (his words), Corbett was trying not to puke, and Evann was relaxed as she took it all in. With a cigarette in one hand and the other on the wheel, the driver hit the gas and whipped down a series of switchbacks. Mountains were to my left, and sea cliffs to my right. It happened before I could comprehend what was going on. I'm a thrill seeker, but our chances of plummeting down a cliff were higher than I liked. I cinched my fanny pack with our passports tight around my waist; it would be easier to identify our bodies after a terrible crash. Meanwhile, Chris, Breese, and Hudson slept through it all. I had trained my children since birth to sleep anywhere, but this was not what I had in mind.

About fifteen minutes later, we arrived at our destination unscathed, grabbed gyro pitas for lunch near our Airbnb, and picked up ingredients to make a chocolate-chip-cookie cake. Our "normal" day abroad was far from what it had been at home.

The Albanian Riviera

From our new apartment balcony, I soaked in the sacred details of the street. The more of the world

and its people I saw, the more I was convinced of its overwhelming goodness. A senior man in a fedora walked up and down the street with his cane. Across the way, a woman reclined on her balcony, sipping her coffee. A priest pulled on a long rope to ring the church bell. A couple of backpackers stood waiting for the next bus out of town, which reminded me we had to figure out how to leave this quiet beach town too.

We spent our days in slow motion between the laid-back streets and hiking to secluded beaches. We made daily visits to a gyro shop for cheap sandwiches and conversations with a sassy teenage employee.

Nearby, a school with a basketball court lured my guys to play. Everett missed a half-court shot, and the ball bounced into the open bathroom window of a closed hardware store. After looking for help and making hand motions to neighbors, Hudson climbed through the window to retrieve it. I don't know if it was the only illegal trespassing of the trip, but it was the first.

Colorful beach umbrellas dotted the nearby shore, and we noticeably stuck out, trying to curl up in the shade of our three little black rain umbrellas. Toward the end of our week, an older couple jumped up to get my attention. I had seen them the previous two days but had not interacted other than with a friendly smile. The man grabbed two beach umbrellas he had tucked against a wall, smiled, and said, "Use these. Free." I responded, "*Faleminderit!* Thank you!" They were weathered; I guessed he might have seen someone leave them behind, and he thoughtfully tucked them away for us.

Between the beach and our apartment, a bakery beckoned us daily with gelato, cookies, cheesecake, and Wi-Fi access. Breese rushed into the apartment one evening, declaring, "My night just got made!" I instantly knew it must have involved the bakery. Food is her love language. She stopped in with some change to buy a single cookie. The owner refused to take her *lek* and sent her on her way with a cookie. Every day in Albania, someone went out of their way to show thoughtfulness and kindness toward us.

WISDOM AND WONDER

In Albania, we felt overwhelmingly welcomed. We did our best to learn about the things we didn't understand—the complexities of history, culture, politics, and current challenges. Ultimately, we could gain only a superficial understanding. Our perspective and feelings toward Albania became rooted in how the people made us feel.

Being guests in new countries, especially Albania, caused us to imagine how international travelers might feel visiting US landmarks or walking down Main Street in our town. There is a big difference between simply accepting someone and an arms-open-wide, big-smile-on-your-face welcome, like the kind Albanians offered us. We want to be a family that does the second.

Cultural Insights

While visiting the capital, we shared coffee with a man who casually said, "Albania is not a culture where time equals money." He was speaking of cultural differences he noticed between the United States and Albania and how he believed most in the United States had plenty when it came to material things but lacked when it came to time to savor life and community. From his perspective, Americans were always so busy running around, hustling, working, and filling up any slice of margin in their schedules that they had no time for lingering at tables, slowly sipping coffee with friends, or connecting daily with others. Of course, his perspective was from a distance, but it still challenged us to ask ourselves what kind of wealth we intentionally wanted to build.

Budget Travel: Use Public Transportation

Decisions for most everything (food, lodging, transportation, and so forth) went through two questions: What is available? Of the available options, what is the cheapest? After those two questions, we considered other factors. This approach meant most of our travel involved public transportation. Instead of being isolated in private vehicles or surrounded by things geared toward tourists, we were on the path of residents, which directly impacted our perceptions and experiences in each place. Public transportation can be unpredictable and tricky to figure out, but it is essential to keep in mind the form of transportation used impacts more than a budget.

Your Adventure

Do I have opportunities to give up my own comfort or even something that is my right for the good of someone else?

GREECE

Fifteen minutes from our destination, the driver I hired to get us across the Albania-Greece border jerked into an abrupt U-turn. Crossing borders was easy. Figuring out what drivers were doing was far more complex. He arrived late to pick us up, and the couple hours of margin I had planned to catch our bus disappeared. With every translation app open on his phone, Chris tried talking to our Albanian driver, our previous host (who spoke Albanian), and the Greek bus company we booked to figure out how to get us to the station on time. However, the language barrier won. We missed the bus.

After his U-turn, the driver motioned us to get out and stand beside the quiet four-lane highway. Getting an explanation of what was going on seemed futile, and we had grown accustomed to being kicked out of vans and buses. It was comical by that point. The sparkling blue sky matched the driver's polo shirt, and his sunglasses hid whether he was stressed. Our best guess was he contacted the bus company and arranged a pickup along its route. In a worst-case scenario, we'd be without a ride several hours from our apartment in Thessaloniki.

We squeezed beside each other on the curb under the shade of a solitary bush. Every travel day, we had asked the same question: "Will we make it?" And despite missed buses, long walks, and canceled flights, we always made it. I could help set the tone for our family, but that was about it. We were

in Greece, after all—that alone was incredible! Sure enough, the driver stood in the middle of the road, arms flailing as he waved down an oncoming bus.

Thessaloniki— a Foodie's Dream

Thessaloniki, a port city on the Aegean Sea with a view of Mount Olympus breaking the horizon, is encompassed by mountains. It would be our home for a week, and as with most destinations, we promptly searched out a basketball court and a grocery store, both found within two blocks of our stay. Selecting yogurt in Greece took more work than navigating its buses. I was overwhelmed by the possibilities and my inability to read any labels. I grabbed a variety. One with a goat, one with a cow, one with a sheep—the animal graphics were the only thing I understood. I laughed at myself, thinking, *This is quite literally all Greek to me.*

The city reminded me of Rome, with ancient buildings erupting around every corner. My older kids rushed past an arch built in AD 298 to follow Evann into a Lego store. A walking street filled with Roman ruins cut through apartments, restaurants, and cafés. We stopped by a gyro shop, and the owner called out to Chris, "Hey! Good to see you again!" With confusion on our faces, we stared Chris down. His earlier search for Wi-Fi had taken a detour, and the owner just busted him for eating without us. When we tasted the gyros, we somewhat forgave Chris—they were the best ones of the trip.

The path between the heart of town and our row house in the suburbs took us through a college campus. We found ourselves caught up in a peaceful protest for the third time. The first was near the Colosseum in Rome, and the second was in Genoa. Protests are not inherently dangerous and have been an effective way of advocating for change for centuries. I am always grateful for the chance to learn about the things people use their voices to speak up about,

and I am thankful for the opportunities to talk about those often-controversial topics with my family.

Sticking to our routine of basketball and bakeries, Breese sampled all the desserts and decided the locally famed cream-filled puff pastry *trigona panoramatos* was her favorite. The guys continued pickup basketball games, gaining new friends and getting the kind of glimpses into a culture only fellow teenagers can provide. In between ancient walls, college students dominated cafés, and older adults made the sign of the cross as they passed a church. It reminded me of smaller university towns in the Midwest, full of the vibrancy of youth but seasoned with nostalgia.

My context for the city had been from the letters in the Bible that Paul wrote to the church in the town. It was the first time we stood in a place mentioned in the Bible, which was fascinating and powerful. Gazing out at sea, Mount Olympus, and the fortified walls, I attempted to envision what life was like when Paul wrote to the Thessalonians, "Always be joyful. Never stop praying. Be thankful in all circumstances."

The "About Your Host" section in the Airbnb listing mentioned the host enjoyed meeting travelers. I figured it would be a fantastic way to learn about Greece, so before thinking it through, I extended an invitation for dessert. Panic set in when I realized I had no idea about the cultural norms for hosting. It was too late; he accepted the invitation. I bought cookies from the neighborhood bakery, canned soda, and tea. "Hi! Welcome to your home. Come on in," I nervously said as I opened the door. He brought with him a bottle of wine and a shy smile. I learned it is a bit uncomfortable to host someone in their home in a country that is not my own. On the flip side, comfort is way overrated. It was a sweet evening of sharing stories and shortbread cookies.

> Gazing out at sea, Mount Olympus, and the fortified walls, I attempted to envision what life was like when Paul wrote to the Thessalonians, "Always be joyful. Never stop praying. Be thankful in all circumstances."

A Strike Kept Us Out

The spotless floors, empty cars, and pristine paint of the five-hour train from Thessaloniki to Athens were a welcomed change from old buses and cramped vans. We exited the train and immediately purchased Athens metro cards for the coming week. Based on prior research, they were our most budget-friendly travel option. Moments later, we found out there would be a city-wide twenty-four-hour public transportation strike. International travel requires a certain amount of humor. Chris and I shrugged it off with the confidence that, like clumsy ballerinas, we could still make a pivot beautiful.

Personal cars and massive parking lots fill our town; the strike opened the door to discuss topics less familiar, like unions, reasons for walkouts, and how public transportation affects many communities. Our Airbnb was a couple blocks from the station, outside the hustle and bustle of the city. Staying off the train meant more time at the nearby basketball court, finding another fantastic gyro shop, and discovering the neighborhood. After a day, we felt at home. Fortune favored the fluid.

With a cane for stability and curly salt-and-pepper hair brushing his shoulders, our new host warmly greeted us. He assured me I didn't have to worry about my family being too loud, because we were in Greece and the Greeks were loud. We needed convincing; our neighborhood in Thessaloniki was nearly silent. Showing us around the apartment, he paused to note his surprise that we, a family from the center of the United States, picked Athens as a destination for a family trip.

His genuine joy that we chose to be in his home on the outskirts of Athens instead of the famous Greek islands was evident. It was a reminder of the value of celebrating the places others call home. As we unpacked bags in our upstairs apartment, he shouted from downstairs that freshly squeezed juice awaited us—his hospitality carried through the open kitchen window.

Athens—Lost in Awe

Once the strike was over, we caught the metro into the city's heart. Athens captivated me within moments of stepping out of the station. It reminded me of other cities we'd visited, yet was markedly different. I loved its grit, open-air markets, bold street art, classical treasures, and *souvlaki*. Tables brimming with hats and souvenirs stood in front of structures built centuries before the United States became a country.

Walking streets that felt like a playground, I feasted on the details spilling out of every nook and cranny. Each view led to a new question. I was more grateful for the prompting of curiosity than I was concerned about knowing the answers. Surrounding me in graffiti and street art were opposing views, challenges to my perceptions, and chances to grow.

I'm a straight, constant line with no extremes, just level—until I land in a city I've never been to. Then, encountering the unknown, my steady line spikes drastically upward. I entered Athens with fresh eyes and childlike wonder. People have discovered the city for thousands of years, but it was my first time. Instead of checking off a list, we walked through the streets and got lost in the city, acutely aware of being wholly alive.

We turned down a side street and jockeyed to cross before an oncoming bus. Glancing to my left, I realized the road ended at a hill with the Parthenon on top. It soared above the city as if the Greek gods had reached down and placed it on the landscape the same way my boys created Lego cities as kids. To my right, charming cafés served up pastries and coffee.

We followed the street toward the Acropolis and Parthenon. Often seen as an icon of democracy, a symbol of the beginnings of Western civilization, and the epitome of ancient Greece, it was mind-boggling to climb the steps of the Parthenon and walk among its ruins and olive trees. Built over two thousand years ago as a temple to Athena, it had been a Byzantine church, Catholic cathedral, mosque, and more. Rocked by earthquakes and fire, plundered, bombed, and damaged by faulty restoration attempts, it still stood.

Scaffolding surrounded sections of the Parthenon. Bright white marble fit like a jigsaw puzzle with the darkened, aged sections. Chunks of carved stone with identification numbers etched into them lined the perimeter in massive piles. Restoration was an ongoing and debated process. Exploring the complex, we approached the remains of the Erechtheion, an arresting building with statues of six women serving as support pillars. They looked strangely familiar. Staring up at their grandeur, I realized a restaurant from my childhood had replicas of the statues, known as caryatids. All those years, I had no idea of their significance. I cared only about my dinner.

A Stranger's Van and the NBA

A connection with another mom on Instagram led to an invitation for my oldest four to hang out with a group of ex-pat teens from around the world. I had sparse details, but my kids were curious and excited to see where it led. After months of conversation primarily limited to family, a night with English-speaking peers was a welcomed break. The longer we were gone, the more deeply they learned what it was like to be the visitor, lessons I knew they'd carry home.

They caught the metro back to our apartment later that night and came through the door, bursting with energy. When we remember Athens, I think of what it looked and felt like; my kids remember the night they jumped in a stranger's van and spent an evening playing games with teens who call countless countries home.

After their late night out, we ventured far from tourist spots to another NBA star's home court. While we missed out on more well-known sites in Athens and Greece, the sidelines of a run-down basketball court contained just as much beauty to savor.

Giannis Antetokounmpo started on the neighborhood court when his family lived in Athens as refugees. After playing a few games, we stopped by the café across the street, where the owners had known the basketball star since he was a little boy. They beamed, chatting about him. Their words focused more on his admirable character than his athletic skills. Our visit gave context to his story and was a springboard for conversations about the complexities of migration, immigration, the plight of refugees, and the challenges countries and communities face considering all three.

Combining personal interests and fun with opportunities to broaden the perspectives of my family ranks ridiculously high on my list of very favorite things in life. It was a big reason I dreamed of this trip for so long.

Under the Twinkle Lights

With our time together ending, our hosts invited us to their patio oasis for our final night in Greece. We'd fly out in the morning, our first flight since arriving in Italy a few months earlier, but before we left, an evening of lingering. Nestled between their row home and the neighbors', our hosts created a paradise filled with plants, hammocks, twinkling lights, and a table for gathering.

She lit candles on the outdoor table, her gentle smile greeting us. He carried another pitcher of freshly squeezed juice (as Breese hoped he would). An avid traveler, he had written books about his adventures and stored in their attic the slides documenting his journeys. Their presence was a gift. They had just returned from burying her sister (after forty days of mourning) and had both recently received a difficult medical diagnosis. As a result of COVID, this was the first night in three years they had welcomed travelers to join them around their table, a practice that had long been a part of their joy in hosting guests.

I'll always wonder what prompted them to invite us to the garden as their first guests after a trying season. We talked about the difficulties and joys of life, the challenges of different countries, the new Italian president, and how the region would change if the European Union collapsed. They shared about "exotic Tulsa" and how the song "Get Your Kicks on Route 66" inspired a dream road trip across the United States. We hoped their dream would come true and we'd have the gift of welcoming them into our home next. Based on films, they believed that no one in America sped when driving, because we have so many police who would approach a speeding car with a gun and potentially put the driver in jail. We assured them that most Americans do, in fact, speed (except me—I hate paying extra for things). Under the glow of strung lights with the most memorable company, our time in Greece ended perfectly.

WISDOM AND WONDER

If calm, cool, and collected were a city, it would be Athens. She reminded me of an eccentric, well-traveled grandma with flowing gray hair, a couple of tattoos, and a boho skirt. She gathered children and adults around her as she told the stories you lean forward in your chair to hear. Her history was wildly long, yet she was defined by more than her past. Her wrinkles made her stunning, and her adventures made her legendary. In my sunset years, I want to be Athens.

Cultural Insights

From Areopagus (Mars Hill), the Acropolis and miles of city in every direction come into view. Waiting among the small crowd that slowly began to form for sunset, I thought of all the events the ground below my feet had held. Once an ancient courtroom and the location of Paul's sermon in Acts 17, this historical site now served as a backdrop for couples on dates as the day faded and for teenagers making TikTok videos in the middle of everyone. Everett wandered off to sit alone and immerse himself in the moment. On the same rocks that he found solitude, mythology says the Greek gods tried Ares for the murder of Poseidon's son. A time-lapse panorama of the millenniums of history from the small hill in the Mediterranean would tell the most fascinating story.

Travel Tip:
Book Based on Review Details

The reviews on booking apps and platforms are a gold mine of information. Before making reservations, I scoured the reviews specifically for insights on the hosts, the neighborhood, and the general feel of the location. I booked many of our stays based on what I read about the hosts or the people who lived in the area and only reserved a couple specifically for their comfort. We weren't on vacation but on a journey to experience the world and its people. Our most memorable experiences in a country were directly related to our hosts or the neighborhood.

Your Adventure

Where was the last place you visited that made all your senses come alive?

BREESE
age twelve at the start of the trip

I clearly remember the feeling of arriving in Morocco. We hopped on the bus from the airport to the city center of Marrakech. Hot, sweaty, and squashed between my brothers, I was happy to be in a place I'd never been, not knowing where I was or even where I was going. We wandered through an alley and passed by spice shops, leather shops, little bakeries, flying mopeds, beautiful buildings, and large, detailed doors. The sun was shining, and I couldn't stop smiling. The adventure was my favorite—not knowing anything, wandering in a new town, seeing how other people live and their values. I also learned more about the life I wanted to live.

Being lost in discovery and beautifully confused is my favorite part of traveling. Some days of our trip were hard. I got sick of it and wanted my bed. I missed good ol' American queso and was tired of zombie apocalypse conversations with my brothers. I missed my friends, my extended family, and my independence. Most of the time, my parents wouldn't let me wander around a town in a foreign country, at least not without a brother, but I got my solo adventures a couple of times. One year of traveling and everything being perfect isn't reality. There were ups and downs, but learning to find peace while waiting for the ups and pushing through the hard of the downs has impacted me every day since returning home.

I can't think of anything that excites me more or gives me more wonder and joy than to be in a country where I'm ignorant of almost everything and only have a basic sense of how things work. Places where I can't read anything or understand what people are saying, and most of the time, the only way to talk is through hand motions and smiles. Being in a crowd of people in a new country is my favorite. Smiling, welcoming faces, loud and busy, everyone is going their separate ways—and so much good-smelling food (oh my gosh, the best part). It made me realize how small I am and showed me how everyone is important and plays a role in the world. Each person plays an instrument that makes the song of life beautiful. Traveling gave me a broader perspective of that song and made me want to hear every little part of it.

People are the best part of travel. I will always remember the hotel bakers in Croatia, my Filipino besties in Argao, and the young woman at the Theth visitors' center (Albania) who shared her lunch with me. Hearing perspectives I'd never heard changed the way I thought and challenged what I believed. Traveling slowed everything down, made me enjoy life, and led to lingering at tables because I had nowhere to be. My heart races when I travel, but I am also completely at peace.

Since the day we got home, I've learned more about wanderlust and have been ready to leave again. Until then, trips to the Asian market have become a biweekly adventure. I feel most at home in other cultures, learning about the wonders of God's beautiful creations.

TÜRKIYE

The street was busy with men and kids running back and forth between a little one-aisle shop and the tall, stacked homes common in Istanbul. Like always, we garnered a handful of stares as we stood trying to find the house we rented. After some confusion and waiting, our host arrived to let us in, point out a few things, and introduce us to our neighbors for the week. Exhausted from a day of buses and a flight from Athens, we quickly tried to settle in for the night.

The home was a traditional Ottoman wood design—over one hundred years old, two stories tall, and featuring shared exterior walls. Leaning out the top floor window, I felt like I could reach across the sidewalk to the dilapidated home across the way. It looked abandoned, with a soccer ball forgotten among cardboard scraps on a curved corner balcony.

The sun had long since set, but the summer heat made sweat drip down my back. We lifted the ridiculously heavy windows for a breeze, but gained only an increase in noise. The shouting, music, and talking from the street below were constant. Jealous of those in my family with noise-canceling AirPods, I piled a stack of my clothes on my head and attempted to sleep. It looked like I made a terrible call on the booking.

I always made reservations with free cancellation policies, so we had the option to leave. However, changing accommodations upon a late-night arrival requires tremendous effort and expense for a family that preferred to make do instead of tromping around a city looking for something different. We had decided early on that we wouldn't cancel a stay unless it was a safety concern. We'd deal with it if it was a comfort or preference issue.

From the time my kids were young, I didn't want them to miss out on an opportunity for an unforgettable experience because their standards for comfort were too high. While other moms worked to keep their kids away from germs and bugs, I was more concerned with the skills mine would need if they ever received an epic invite to sleep in a jungle hut with dirt floors, thatched walls, and no water to clean their hands. I wanted them to experience mouth-watering meals and uncommon company without being distracted by a sticky table.

By 3:15 a.m., I questioned all that and wasn't sure how we'd make it a week.

Then morning arrived.

We met more neighbors; almost all were families barely making it financially. Our doorbell rang incessantly with requests for Breese to play. Hudson did card tricks and backflips in the street, creating the best kid chaos. The little girls giggled and surrounded Evann, hoping for her attention. Everett pulled out his basketball, and young boys formed circles with their arms to serve as hoops in the street. A shop owner across the street had an elementary-aged daughter. I never saw her mom. She remembered my name after hearing it only once and always greeted me with a hug.

Our street came to life at night when young men returned from long days of construction work. We adjusted to the noise. We stayed up later and slept in longer. Our little corner was a blip on the map among the streets of one of the world's largest cities. The Turkish kids. The American family. The refugees. The self-proclaimed mafia member from Kyrgyzstan. We were a mixed-up bag of people, a makeshift community for a week. On concrete steps, we shared snacks, sugar-laden tea, and often heartbreaking stories.

Istanbul—a City Spanning Two Continents

Once known as Constantinople and Byzantium, Istanbul was founded sixteen hundred years before New York City. It is the only city in the world that stretches across two continents. We could have breakfast in Europe and enjoy a midmorning coffee in Asia. Our legs burned as we climbed up and

> From the time my kids were young, I didn't want them to miss out on an opportunity for an unforgettable experience because their standards for comfort were too high.

down the city's hills from our neighborhood to the metro stop.

Pointed, domed ceilings of white plaster with red and blue designs kept my eyes turned upward as we entered Istanbul's Grand Bazaar. It is one of the world's oldest covered markets, with over four thousand shops on sixty-one streets. Men with copper trays and glass cups bolted through the crowds, delivering *çay*. Watching, I wondered how those drinking the tea knew where to return their little cups amid the labyrinth of spices, antiques, jewelry, and leather goods. I tried to think of something similar in my own culture and came up empty-handed. The tea delivery at the Grand Bazaar was utterly new and unique. Every employee in the restaurant, vendor in the market, and tea deliverer was male. As I observed my surroundings and snacked on another baklava sampler box Breese convinced her dad to buy, my mind raced with questions.

Weaving through busy streets and navigating crowds, we moved toward two of Istanbul's most famous sites: the Blue Mosque and the Hagia Sophia. There were bus and train options from the bazaar, but time was a commodity we had in abundance, and the slow pace of walking meant more opportunities to savor our surroundings and stop for ice cream.

Separated by a park, the coned minarets of both mosques dominated the skyline. As we entered the Blue Mosque, we removed our shoes and recalled a *Ms. Marvel* episode featuring a mosque shoe thief. After a brief tour, we strolled through the park and Corbett realized the well-worn black Nikes on his feet were not his. We waited while he ran back to the mosque shoe racks to return the shoes he accidentally stole and search for his pair. A perplexed dad was relieved and smiled when Corbett walked up with his Nikes.

As with the churches in Rome, I studied Hagia Sophia during college and was thrilled to see it in person. Rebuilt in 537 after a fire, it was a Christian church and center for Byzantine culture for nearly nine hundred years before becoming a mosque during the Ottoman Empire. For centuries, it had been a place of worship for Christians and Muslims.

The *adhan* filled the air as we made our way out of the towering doors. Before June, I had never heard the Islamic call to prayer, but after months of travel, it had become a familiar sound. Due to their proximity, the Blue Mosque and the Hagia Sophia went back and forth, taking turns reciting the prayer over loudspeakers instead of competing. The unforgettable duet echoed through Sultanahmet Park.

Our wandering led us under laundry hung to dry, stretched across narrow cobbled alleyways. I wondered if neighbors asked each other, "Hey, do you mind putting a hook for my laundry line on the side of your house?" What happened if the neighbor across the way didn't like you? Were they required to let you hang your clothes under their window? Growing up in a town with houses spaced apart and indoor dryers, I had many questions. Chris passed some little guys doing push-ups in the street and challenged them to a competition. An older man sitting on nearby steps laughed at the show of masculinity below a bunting of underwear and shirts.

Our route took us down the famous İstiklal Caddesi, a street flanked on both sides by buildings from the 1800s. We passed stores devoted entirely to baklava and Turkish delight, and in between Starbucks and H&M, a man selling *dondurma* delighted kids by teasing them as he served cones of the stretchy ice cream. Soon, a low beat began to rumble among the crowd. As the drumming increased, I quickly led my kids in chasing down the source of the sound. Moments later, we caught up to a parade. Travel without an itinerary makes room for endless happy accidents.

During our time in Istanbul, I listened to a podcast in which the host stated, "You and everyone you know will be dead soon. What are you going to

go around caring about?" I found myself under a canopy of rainbow umbrellas, sipping tea with my family at a little café, and pondering those words. A morbid sentiment for some, it was for me a compelling reminder to make sure I was spending my days, however long or short they may be, caring about the right things.

Getting caught up in what others value, devote time to, and even fear is easy. It takes a lot of intention and mindfulness to avoid adopting someone else's list as my own. Surrounded by the sights and sounds of Türkiye, I cared about living a full day, taking risks, and loving those around me well—my family, strangers, and the refugee neighbors we had grown to love. It was an easy practice to adopt a thousand miles from responsibilities and obligations. It was more challenging at home.

Cappadocia—Fairy Chimneys and Hot-Air Balloons

Wrapped in blankets and with bleary eyes, we climbed to the rooftop terrace for sunrise. The vast tan landscape camouflaged low-lying buildings in the same shade. As the sun rose, it illuminated a hundred hot-air balloons that daily filled the sky and floated above the fairy chimneys, the otherworldly and magnificent cone-shaped rock formations famous in Cappadocia. We waved at passengers in crowded baskets as they passed overhead. It didn't feel real standing on that little roof and looking over at my family.

Balloons began launching in the region in the '80s (or '90s, depending on your source) and take off every morning weather permits. The balloon rides are a big draw to the towns in the Cappadocia region, but the people who visited only to ride a balloon or chase down an Instagram-worthy photo missed so much the area offered.

Located in central Türkiye, Cappadocia is home to hundreds of cave churches carved into the region

> The ever-changing home base and lack of routine had once sounded exhausting but now was becoming a source of deep rest and a profound awakening to life.

... during the ninth and tenth centuries by Byzantine Christians. While the most preserved were in open-air museums, others filled the valleys and were only to be discovered while hiking. So, we hiked. And we hiked. And we hiked—for miles among the rocky chimneys and pillars jutting up from the barren plateau. It was astonishing to climb through an opening in a rock, step inside, and find the remains of a church with thousand-year-old frescoes of saints painted on the walls and ceilings.

Usually, adding a human touch takes away from the magnificence of nature in a place. Cappadocia felt different. The erosion by nature followed by the carving out of civilizations by people created a mysterious and distinctive landscape. Instead of blocky homes with mass-manufactured elements, the structures followed the organic lines of the terrain and the rocks they were etched inside. It was like wind and man danced together, and walking around, we could witness the artistry of both.

Back in town, we stuck to the outskirts, where we found a grocery store that sold Oreo ice cream bars for thirty-three cents each. We had an unofficial family rule: I'd agree to the splurge if the ice cream was a dollar or less. With a single bar costing only thirty-three cents, my kids used their debate skills to get me to comply with three bars each. It was far more than they needed, and I felt ridiculous at the checkout buying nineteen ice cream bars (three for the rest, one for me). However, when asked about top trip memories, my kids always bring up the thirty-three-cent Oreo bars among the sand towers of Cappadocia.

Walking out of the motel on our last morning, we climbed through a dozen twentysomething backpackers collapsed on the steps outside—large bags strewn about acted as makeshift pillows. The sun had yet to rise, and the new arrivals looked thrashed, waiting for the check-in time. I'll never forget the confusion on their faces as our family walked out with backpacks half the size of the ones they carried. We bewildered the young backpacker crowd everywhere we went.

Now and then, I'd catch a glimpse of our reflection on the side of a building, and I'd be surprised too. We were past the season of being homesick and had settled into days full of promise and unknown possibilities. Somewhere along the way, everything started feeling normal, natural, and just right. The ever-changing home base and lack of routine had once sounded exhausting but now was becoming a source of deep rest and a profound awakening to life.

WISDOM AND WONDER

Sitting in our Airbnb in Istanbul, as I listened to Chris and the men on our street laughing outside in the darkness, I simultaneously scrolled through messages from the United States that popped up on my phone. One implored us to be safe in our travels in Türkiye while another revealed gunshots had rung out in my hometown at a high school football game. Hudson noticed two teenagers outside the window digging through trash bins, looking for items to sell for recycling, and he commented that it was tough knowing how to respond to his friends back home when they lamented not getting the latest consumer or fashion trend. We were all struggling to make sense of what we were experiencing in light of messages about safety and material wants from home.

Chris and I knew we were making life harder for our kids, not because they were far from home and sleeping at a two-star Airbnb on uncomfortable beds. We were making it more complicated because growth can be painful, and they were growing in empathy and understanding. They would have to figure out how to reconcile what they learned with their lives and life back home.

Cultural Insights

By the entrance to a remote cave church stood a juice stand with three umbrella-covered tables and an expansive view of the valley below—the owner, an outgoing beekeeper, self-appointed himself the church's protector. We sipped freshly squeezed pomegranate juice, Sprite, peach tea, and Cokes as he taught us about the valley, the caves, and the area's churches.

A couple of times, fellow hikers passed by us. "Hello! There is a beautiful church up here!" he called out. Some waved back, but most ignored him. In their haste or fear of a charge or scam, they missed all they could have gained from lingering at his table and witnessing the frescos in the church. It was hard to watch. In our travels, I hoped my kids would experience places like ancient cave churches, but I wanted them equally (if not more) to sip drinks at tables with people of far different life experiences and learn their stories.

Family Travel: Decide Together

Our initial plans for Cappadocia included a hot-air balloon, but we quickly realized those in our budget packed twenty-four-plus people in a basket. If we got stuck in the middle, we wouldn't be able to see. It would be a huge expense, equal to nearly two months of our food budget, without guaranteeing we could enjoy it.

As a family, we discussed our options and chose to put the funds toward future adventures. A balloon ride that did not involve being squished would have been spectacular, but my kids were learning to make decisions based on personal priorities and not what everyone else did or recommended.

Your Adventure

Are you more inclined to see beauty in people or landscapes? Do you believe it can be found in both?

JORDAN

"Whoa!" the customs agent exclaimed with a delighted laugh. While stamping my passport, he realized we not only had five kids but had traveled to Jordan with them too. A few other officers came over—all grinning, announcing, "Welcome to Jordan," and reveling in the big stack of passports. It was 2:45 a.m., and they were full of energy and possibly strong tea. Our middle-of-the-night arrival was made unexpectedly sweet by their friendliness.

The jet-black sky engulfed us as we drove our rental van from the airport for hours through the arid countryside toward two cheap rooms at a guesthouse with solid reviews. As the paved road turned to gravel, which turned to dust, I wondered, *What did I get us into this time?* For months, my family joked about the sketchiness of some of my plans. A dark, remote road in Jordan was no exception. However, as the sun rose, it revealed an expansive view of the Jordan River Valley right outside our door. My kids could poke fun at my planning all they wanted, but they had to admit that they ended up in a better-than-best possible scenario nine times out of ten.

After a few hours of sleep in our surprisingly spacious rooms, we drove to the nearby one-street town for lunch. Sitting in a *shawarma* shop, a group of middle-school-aged boys walked in after school. They quickly overcame the shock of seeing us by challenging my guys to arm wrestling matches. Cheers and laughter erupted from those grilling meat as the tests of strength spoke words the language barrier blocked. In impulsive excitement, one kid invited us to his house for dinner. We laughed and told him it might surprise his mom if seven Americans showed up for *mansaf*. I imagined my response if Everett walked into our kitchen with a Jordanian family he met while grabbing an after-school snack. I adore middle school boys and the ways they think (or don't think).

Our host invited us to have "Jordanian Whiskey" (*shai*/tea) under a pavilion on the guesthouse grounds lined by olive trees overlooking the Dead Sea. We chatted about his childhood growing up in Palestine, life in Jordan as a refugee, diplomatic relations with Saudi Arabia, and US politics. He asked my opinion of women's rights in Iran, and I pressed him on what it is like having a king. He wondered if there are countries that all Americans hate. I explained that *fear* is a better word than *hate*. My kids were growing up in an American culture increasingly defined and motivated by fear, isolation, and self-preservation. Messages that the world was on fire and unsafe dominated the news and social media. I paused, then told him we were on this trip to show our kids the opposite. He tilted his head, smiled, and dropped too much sugar in our tea, letting us know Jordanians like their tea extra sweet.

We spent our last night with our host, the owner, and ten of his male friends, savoring grilled chicken, rice, yogurt, and french fries. After dinner, my guys joined the business leaders, doctors, and professors around a patio firepit, sipping endless cups of tea and mindlessly eating finger-size desserts like baklava. With genuine curiosity, they grilled Corbett, Hudson, and Everett on homeschooling and education in the United States. They found common ground on the importance of education and the freedom to pursue knowledge. When my guys gathered with them for a group photo, Hudson's blond hair and teal shirt stood out in the center, surrounded by men wearing

dishdashas (long robes for men) and *shemagh* (red-and-white-checkered head coverings). As a family, we affectionately refer to that night as "The Meeting of the Minds."

Wadi Rum—Cave Camping

Piled back in the van, we drove south on the King's Highway, a five-thousand-year-old route that ran through Jordan. It led us to the barren wild of Wadi Rum, where I booked a few nights of camping with a Bedouin host. Bordering Saudi Arabia and on the edge of the Arabian Desert, it was a vast expanse of crimson sand. Gigantic rocks randomly scattered about looked as if a child playing in a sandbox tossed them in the air. I was confident Mars looked the same.

"How big is the cave? Is there a bathroom? What are we going to eat?" my family asked. "I don't know—I've never been here before." I had fully embraced my new favorite response and the freedom of not having answers. We pulled into a parking lot, where our guide picked us up in his double-decker SUV. A solid welding job created rooftop seating. It was a playpen on wheels for those open to a bit of risk, which included my crew. As we drove through a tiny village on the outskirts, I noted the absence of women.

A knee-high stone wall enclosed three sides of the campsite, nestled in the crevice of a granite and sandstone hill. Woven blankets and cushions created a sofa in the sand. A brass kettle whistled in a small firepit. Our guide pointed toward a concrete structure at the end of a long path, noting it was the bathroom. I sighed with relief. The online listing did not mention a campsite bathroom. Though I knew everyone had the same basic needs, I wasn't sure how they'd be met in a highly primitive setting. In the months leading up to our stay, I had envisioned a bucket in the corner of a cave and me hovering over it under a blanket in the middle of the night. A long walk under the stars was far better than the bucket

option. As our guide welcomed us with Bedouin coffee—a dark black roast with cardamom—we tossed our backpacks in the sand.

Under the stars and with phone flashlights, we watched layered metal trays being pulled out of underground barrels. They reminded me of the tiered trays people in the US put on their kitchen islands with cupcakes, but these were much bigger and used to cook our dinner. Deep contentment fell over me as I gazed at my kids diving into a meat and vegetable feast with four other guests and our host.

I laughed listening to them make jokes about stereotypes with a young man from the United Kingdom, who readily shared his obsession with US cowboy culture and rodeos. Two European women in their twenties rounded out our group. In southern Jordan's barren landscape, my kids found themselves eating new foods and swapping stories as peers with fellow adventure chasers. Music, games, sugar-laden tea, and desserts continued until our eyes could no longer stay open. Our bodies lined up under thick blankets and the stars. The concept of a silence so fierce it was deafening made sense for the first time. In Istanbul, I wondered if I could fall asleep to the noise. In Wadi Rum, the silence and its strange combination of eerie and serene kept me alert.

Jolted awake by phone alarms, we climbed boulders to watch the sunrise. Glowing pinks and reds replaced the daytime browns of the sand. It was spectacular. Our guide's cousin arrived to take us exploring in his double-decker truck. The lack of doors and windows invited us to hang off the back end and sides. With the wind whipping our hair, we bounced through the sand, stopping to learn history. Among etchings two thousand years old, a primitive carving of a mother standing and giving birth caught my attention. Aside from the two Europeans, she was the first woman I saw in Wadi Rum.

In between sandboarding and rock climbing, questions flooded my mind about the history of the area and its people. The harsh conditions and barren landscape held tremendous significance for millenniums.

> When flashlights and lanterns died, we embraced the silence and darkness to witness the Milky Way igniting the sky. Was this what Abraham experienced? This sand and these stars?

Some believe it was where Moses crossed the Red Sea and led his people in the days of wandering in the desert. Others point to it being the setting of the book of Job and the possible location where Abraham, a figure central to the world's three monotheistic religions (Judaism, Islam, Christianity), looked to the sky as God told him his descendants would outnumber the stars.

The sun sank and we returned to the campsite. A phone flashlight propped on a water bottle served as a spotlight for dinner and games. Our eyes grew big when the conversation turned to 2020 and our guide recounted treasure hunting among the sand, rocks, and dunes. We envisioned him on a camel disappearing into the desolate terrain for something buried long ago. The whole world went through the isolation and trauma of COVID lockdowns, and the way he spent it was by far the most exciting we had heard. When flashlights and lanterns died, we embraced the silence and darkness to witness the Milky Way igniting the sky. Was this what Abraham experienced? This sand and these stars?

It struck me how my kids seemed utterly unaware of

the abnormality of their lives. They slept in the desert, eating food cooked in the sand with strangers like it was what every high schooler did during the fall semester. Even stranger, it felt totally normal to me too. Many back home considered this sliver of the world volatile, dangerous, and unsafe. I dug my toes in the sand and wondered what my kids' thoughts would be when someone mentioned the Arabian Desert. Would they remember learning games from our Bedouin guide or how their mom killed it at sandboarding? Would they remember the British backpacker obsessed with American cowboys or the people's hospitality? Different elements would stand out to each of them, but I knew their perspectives would be ones of familiarity and fondness—a far cry from what headlines provided.

Petra—an Indiana Jones Birthday

As a child of the '80s and a fan of Harrison Ford, I arranged our schedule to be in Petra—the epic backdrop for *Indiana Jones and the Last Crusade*—for my birthday. There were a few ways to explore Petra. I picked a route that was the least convenient but with no crowds and the most uncomfortable but also the most adventurous. We'd hike more than seven miles through the backcountry and onto a path leading to the well-known areas of Petra instead of entering a mile away at the visitor center. My crew agreed to this plan—mainly because it was my birthday.

We pulled up to our Airbnb in a tiny village north of Petra. Tarps and fabrics secured by ropes formed the rooftops of several nearby structures. A couple of donkeys and a horse tied next to a door marked our destination on Google Maps. The *adman* bellowed over loudspeakers and filled the khaki-colored landscape. A Jack Sparrow look-alike arrived and introduced himself as our host. With waist-length black dreads covered with a blue bandanna, he wore cargo pants, military-style boots, a stack of bracelets, rings, and a tan button-up shirt. His thick black eyeliner was an Arab tradition thousands of years old, with deep historical, religious, and cultural ties. I came from a country with "One-Hundred-Year-Old Historical Home" markers. The earliest records of the entirety of human history were rooted to the very landscapes outside our window.

With Wadi Rum sand still in our hair, the ideal night for my kids included showers, Netflix, and hang time. Chris and I opted to drive the fifteen minutes to Petra's main tourist town, Wadi Musa, to buy hiking snacks and research where to park the rental car during the hike. The more we could figure out ahead of time, the smoother things always went. Knowing we'd have some hungry and tired teens on our hands, we needed things to be easy once we finished the hike. When I saw the streets lined with expensive restaurants and overpriced souvenir stalls, I was immensely grateful we booked our stay a few miles away at a place with donkeys instead of in a town catering to tourists. Our wallets were thankful too.

Our hike began at dawn among the two-thousand-year-old buildings carved in sandstone at Siq al-Barid, also known as Little Petra. The early arrival meant we were alone to wind through the carvings and up narrow passages for 360-degree views of the barren landscape extending to the horizon in every direction. For the next several hours, we sometimes followed a footpath and sometimes hoped we'd find the path we had lost. At one point, a local man walking his donkeys started yelling, "Petra!" and pointed us in a different direction. We had no idea where he came from, but he saved us a lot of sweat and frustration by putting us on the correct path.

As we hiked through the isolated landscape, it seemed impossible that an entire civilization had existed anywhere nearby. When we spotted the top of the Monastery, an intricately carved structure soaring 154 feet in the air, we felt like modern-day explorers stumbling on an archaeological wonder hidden by time. Indiana Jones made Petra's Treasury famous as he dove through the perfectly carved columns, escaping death in the final scene, but the Monastery was equally impressive. We continued on dusty paths through the rest of the UNESCO site with eyes wide in disbelief and astonishment, heading in the opposite direction of the crowds and exploring some of the five hundred buildings still standing. Named one of the New Seven Wonders of the World in 2007, Petra's construction without modern tools stunned and baffled us.

All our sidetracked wandering turned our seven-mile hike into a nine-mile adventure. With our snack bag depleted and another mile to go, we walked quickly and avoided talking to Breese, whose hunger was overtaking her usually upbeat demeanor. Eventually, we were back in the rental van with snacks and a thoroughly contented daughter eating an ice cream. A part of the world that had been only a movie backdrop came alive. Over the years, Chris knew the way to my heart and had celebrated my birthday by taking me to skydive, to fly open cockpit, to learn trapeze, and now to visit Petra. Hiking among ancient ruins in the desert would be massively hard to beat.

As a family, we welcomed risk, unease, discomfort, and the chance for everything to turn out awful because of the possible what-ifs: What if it works out? What if it is better than we hoped? I've now failed enough times to know things not working according to plan are way less scary than my younger self believed. We weren't sure what to look for when we came to Jordan. Still, a mysterious landscape became familiar, and we found endless "Welcome to Jordan" greetings, cups of tea, and lessons in history, geography, culture, and religion. As an innately curious person, I'd far rather leave a place with a mind full of questions than a camera full of breathtaking pictures. Jordan, however, gifted me with both.

WISDOM AND WONDER

Camping in the desert under the stars with a Bedouin host; floating in the Dead Sea; climbing ancient sandstone civilizations; embracing new people, places, and experiences—Chris and I were doing things that made us feel wildly alive and in sync with each other. Traveling with older teens gave us a tremendous amount of freedom to enjoy our days more as partners than parents. As much as I relished seeing my kids be brave, adventurous, and worry free, I was equally grateful they were witnessing their parents doing the same. They saw us in rare form, freed from the mundane responsibilities and tasks of daily life. We were curious, excited, and effortlessly at ease in every culture. We were the very best version of ourselves, alive and energized experiencing all the wonder together.

Cultural Insights

In Wadi Rum, I asked our guide why I had yet to see any women in the area and intently listened as he shared about the traditions and customs of the Bedouins, specifically aspects of how women stayed within their homes. I longed to sit with women in the area, share a cup of tea, and hear their stories firsthand. A Bedouin man could tell me only so much about being a Bedouin woman. What my eyes saw, my heart felt, and my mind sensed was different from my family's. The speed and diversity at which we traveled allowed me to briefly, yet profoundly, experience places only to be quickly thrust into something different. To experience the world from the perspective of a woman was both beautiful and confusing.

Travel Tip:
Reach Out for Custom Rates

In researching Wadi Rum, I discovered several options for lodging and tours, but none providing exactly what I had in mind. I found a cave camp offering jeep tours for individuals with stellar reviews. Always, always, always read (and leave) reviews. I sent a message asking for the rate of a customized family package including everything I had in mind. The combined cost of two nights' stay, an eight-hour jeep tour, and all our meals was a third of the cheapest one-hour hot-air balloon tour in Cappadocia. When traveling as a group on a budget, reaching out directly to tour guides can lead to better rates than those stated online.

Your Adventure

When you ask yourself, *What if?* is it usually from the perspective of *What if the worst-case scenario happens* or *What if the best-case scenario happens*?

ISRAEL

This visit took place in October 2022. These words were written in August 2023. Events from October 2023 onward are not included.

The weight of the intense sun bore down on us as we jockeyed around the bus shelter for slivers of shade. Chris and I glanced at each other and used Google Lens to translate the intricate Hebraic bus timetable on the wall. Seemingly stranded on the side of the highway in the West Bank just outside the Jordan border crossing, I knew we'd figure things out eventually, but a few hours of waiting sounded miserable.

We squinted at the approaching bus spinning dust on its arrival and celebrated reading its number. As I took my seat, I noticed a young woman about Corbett's age asleep on the nearby bench. Across her lap lay an assault rifle. I assumed the much pricier tourist buses we declined didn't have sleeping soldiers with guns. A quick scan revealed that most of those traveling with us were Israeli conscripts. For the next hour, we'd watch soldiers hop on and off, all with guns in their hands and backpacks over their shoulders. *I'm going to learn a lot over the next week*, I thought.

Jerusalem— Come as You Are

Rain fell as we walked to our hostel and were greeted by a friendly staff member. In colorful block lettering, his shirt read "Come as You Are." They were perfect words of welcome for the diversity of people that wander in with backpacks and stories. After a full day of travel, we decided to stick close for the night.

The game room provided a place to gather with others, cook dinner, and spread out a little. Older adults from northern Europe invited me into their Rummikub game. Breese joined fellow travelers in a hummus-making class. Chris retold stories of his time in China to a woman who called it home. With countless countries and ages represented, this was the most diverse hostel we'd experienced. Everyone, it seemed, made a pilgrimage here.

Hours later, Hudson and Everett returned to our room with lemonades. When I asked where they got the drinks, they said they beat an Israeli security guard at pool and he treated them to drinks at the hostel bar. I was glad it was lemonade!

With only a few days in town, we woke up early to walk to the Old City, home to the revered sites of Judaism, Islam, and Christianity. It was Friday, a holy day for Muslims and the start of Shabbat for Jews. We made our way through the massive Jaffa Gate, one of the eight gates of the walled Old City. Every nook and cranny bore layers of a complex history and complicated present. *I am walking the streets of Jerusalem!* I reminded myself. Little red motorized carts transported goods. Garments and blankets hanging overhead blocked the sun and provided respite in the shade. Tables offered snacking options of fruits and nuts. The deeper we wandered, the more life spilled out around us.

Slowly, we made our way to the Western Wall and the sounds of Jewish worship and celebration. We watched as men rocked back and forth in prayer and listened to the reading of Scripture out loud. Families, full of joy, came together. Devout worshippers in white shirts and black hats stood in contrast to tourists in jeans and T-shirts. Deemed the most sacred site in Judaism, the wall dates to the second century and was all that remained of the Second Temple.

The wall also served as a base for the Dome of the Rock and Al-Aqsa Mosque—the third-holiest site in Islam. The shared wall highlighted the inescapable tension that sometimes felt like it permeated the air more than the smells of *shawarma* roasting. As we began our exit, soldiers flooded the large square due to the protest, unrest, and conflict that had marked Fridays and holidays. There was no commotion, and no one seemed fazed; but as visitors, we found it alarming to see so many men with rifles fill a location of prayer and celebration.

We walked through the gates and toward Kidron Valley, which separates the Mount of Olives and the Old City. Passing the valley's whitewashed tombs, we climbed back up to the Garden of Gethsemane. Filled with olive trees and purple bougainvillea, the garden marks where Jesus spent his final night.

From the Mount of Olives, we gazed out across Jerusalem. The shining gold on the Dome of the Rock demanded attention against the tan and gray cityscape. From our viewpoint, we could see and hear as Muslims began Friday prayers in the mosque courtyard. Out of view, Jews prayed and prepared for Shabbat. And there we were...a Christian family walking paths on a hillside paramount to our faith.

I opened the hostel's window as a siren filled the streets, signaling the coming start of Shabbat. We joined travelers in the game room for a community

dinner. With blessings in Hebrew and raised wine glasses, the communal dinner welcomed an eclectic group of people discovering local culture and each other over traditional food. Between bites of salad and chicken, we traded stories about journeys past and ahead. We were pilgrims in a sacred city, tasting the sweetness of breaking bread at tables lined with diverse diners.

As we visited sites significant to the Christian faith, it was challenging to read through all the layers of history and understand the accuracy of some of the locations, which were often ornate and chaotic with crowds. I wrestled to connect the past to the present. In each place, I'd close my eyes and try to strip away much of what I saw and heard, giving me space to imagine what could have been. While I savored personal moments of reflection and stood in awe of walking where Jesus once did, I could not escape the tension I felt on the streets. It was overwhelming to process.

Of all that a visit to Jerusalem provides, the overlooks and high viewpoints resonated most with me. As a visual learner, I found that walking valleys and climbing hilltops helped me understand the distance between the locations of biblical stories. I've walked from Caiaphas's house to the Mount of Olives. I picture the terrain when I read that story and feel my legs burning while ascending the hill. I've splashed water from the Sea of Galilee on my face and tasted the saltiness of the Dead Sea. I experienced the stories with my senses—the words on the pages will forever read differently.

Hebron—Dual Narratives

Along with ten others and an energetic Jewish guide, we boarded a bus in Jerusalem and began the journey to the West Bank city of Hebron. As part of a dual narrative tour, we would spend half our day with our Jewish guide and the other half with a Muslim Palestinian guide. We could see the Israeli West Bank barrier wall from the bus window. It stood ominous and haunting. Our Jewish guide described it as necessary and began listing reasons he considered it essential. He recited numbers and stats. What he said made sense.

Then he began generalizing about all Palestinians. My kids looked in my direction. We had shared tea and baklava two weeks before in Jordan with a Palestinian father of five born in the West Bank. The words of our guide did not reflect every Palestinian; we knew they also did not reflect the hearts or beliefs of all Jews or Israelis. The tour had barely begun, and we all sensed it would require our utmost attention and discernment.

On our way to Hebron, we passed metal gates, manned checkpoints, and murals. After a summary of the different areas of the city and the controlling parties, we were introduced to our Palestinian guide and headed off to the Tomb of the Patriarchs. The tomb marks the burial location of Abraham, Sarah, Isaac, Rebekah, Jacob, and Leah. It is a sacred and holy site for Islam, Judaism, and Christianity because all three faiths esteem Abraham. The holy site bears the scars of centuries of bloodshed, turmoil, and deep division. With bulletproof glass and bars cutting the building in half (one side for Jews to worship, one side for Muslims), it made peace feel elusive.

From the tomb, we walked the narrow corridors of the Palestinian market in the old city. Cave-like stalls with rock walls displayed handblown glass and earth-tone pottery. Leather bags, woven baskets, Sprite, and antique knickknacks were laid out on little tables and hung overhead.

We ate lunch with our Palestinian guide, all squeezed around his living room table as he shared stories of shuttered stores, dislocated families, and his perspective of a conflict with land at the heart of it. He was the sixth generation of his family to live in his home. He spoke concern for his people, the loss

> We met God in Israel and the West Bank not because we walked where Jesus walked but because we walked with the people he made.

of homes, and what he saw as colonization. The vast border wall we passed on the bus deemed a necessary protection against terrorism by our Jewish guide was a picture of racial segregation and apartheid to our Palestinian guide—very different narratives based on very different experiences in the same land.

We met back with our first guide and returned to the Jewish side of the Cave of the Patriarchs. Peering through the glass and bars, we saw Muslims praying on the other side. We asked questions about what we heard and tried to make sense of the contradictory things spoken. We went on to spend time with Jewish settlers and learned about their longing to live out their faith and lives free from persecution. I held with compassion the collective pain they've felt as a people. For centuries, they've endured tremendous devastation and loss. We sat in a rebuilt synagogue and listened as they recounted stories of deep suffering, dispersion, and their feelings of profound attachment to the land.

Breese leaned over to me and said, "At this point, I have no idea what to think." I nodded in agreement. Our hearts grieved and ached for all the people of this land. We met God in Israel and the West Bank not because we walked where Jesus walked but because we walked with the people he made.

WISDOM AND WONDER

Proximity breeds empathy—we were traveling the world for that reason. We walked Jerusalem's bougainvillea-lined streets and wandered its vibrant markets. We passed Jewish homes with doors open and families laughing inside during Shabbat and got caught up in a crowd of joyful Muslim worshippers leaving Friday prayers at Al-Aqsa Mosque. We played endless games of pool with young Israelis and witnessed bar mitzvah celebrations at the Western Wall. We bought the best baklava from a young girl and her dad in Hebron and ate lunch in a welcoming Palestinian home.

Our homeschooling curriculum had included a few years of studying debate and recognizing argument fallacies. I listened as my sons peppered our guides with questions and challenged what they saw as personal attacks and false dichotomies instead of logic. My kids didn't sit back but engaged fully. At one point, I worried that Hudson might be too intense with his questioning, but at the same time, I felt pride watching him immersed in what he was learning. A few days and a handful of intentional conversations gave us a better context for the news we read, but it would remain only a glimpse. We recognized two very different narratives from two men willing to share their voices and perspectives. We were grateful for seats at their tables.

Cultural Insights

Exploring outside the main tourist hubs in Israel gave us our first experience of being immersed in an Orthodox community. We made mental notes of all the new things we observed, saw, or heard and then took the time to learn more. For instance, while visiting a restaurant near the Sea of Galilee, we watched families tap a small box on the door and kiss their fingers before walking inside for dinner. From that moment on, we paid particular attention to doorframes and how people entered a room. We noticed the same little patterned boxes when we walked down the hallway of our hostel. A quick Google search taught us it was called a *mezuzah* and contained religious texts written on parchment. We repeated this process over and over again. Observation is often the first step in learning.

Travel Tip: Utilize Google Maps

There are several map apps available to help in both planning and traveling. We used Google Maps to create a custom map before our trip and continued to add to it as we traveled. When I found something I wanted to remember (bakery, basketball court, bus station, waterfall, lookout point, and so forth), I added it to our map. Having all our potential ideas in one place made arriving at a new location easy. We also used the option to add details for things we didn't want to forget, like bus numbers to reach the destination or tips I read online.

Your Adventure

What ways can you actively seek out more than one side of a story or situation?

EVERETT
age fourteen at the start of the trip

Sports have brought people together for who knows how long. We experienced them around the ancient sites of Rome, Morocco's dunes, and even Thailand's alleyways. Everywhere in the world, young and older people come together to play sports. Because of this, sports are an excellent way to experience a country's culture. We jumped right in as we traveled, whenever we got the opportunity to join in a game of basketball or soccer. Our trip would have been drastically different without the hundreds of kids who invited us to join their games.

As we traveled through the Philippines, it became clear that basketball was central to their culture. On the coast, there was basketball. In the mountains, there was basketball. In the poorest part of the city, there was basketball. The Filipinos had found something many countries try so hard to find but never can: an activity that brought every person together.

No place symbolized the Filipinos' love of basketball to me more than a small town on the coast. As we walked the dirt paths, we immediately became the talk of the town. "Gringos" were in town, and what better way to meet those gringos than to try to cook them in some friendly basketball competition? There was one surprise: a twenty-peso buy-in to play in any game. We assumed it was to encourage everyone to try and further the competition. The winners made about thirty-five pesos. The remaining five pesos went to the self-appointed referee. We gathered our pesos and joined many games. In the end, out of appreciation for the young Filipinos who had welcomed us, we bought everyone cookies with our earnings.

Basketball seemed to be the same everywhere I went, but how cultures viewed the game changed. Countries like the Philippines, Slovenia, and Greece had more courts and better players because they valued the sport more than others.

How a country played sports and why it valued playing gave us insights into each culture we would have missed otherwise. For instance, America often values sports for entertainment and competition, which correlates directly to American culture. Countries like Thailand and Ecuador play sports as a way to bring their communities together.

Everywhere we visited, locals weren't afraid to invite us in and convince us to join their game, no matter the sport. That hospitality is what I took away the most. As we traveled and found different soccer fields and basketball courts, we received a glimpse into how people lived in that country and gained memories to take home.

EGYPT

The moonlight outlined their guns, but shadows hid the expressions of the border officers. After months of smiles and friendly crossings, our run of positive experiences at borders abruptly ended in Egypt, where a particular agent made the process exasperating. Despite our research, preparation, and knowledge, we eventually gave up, paid more than we should have, and boarded a questionable van in the dark. My plan had included being on a bus under the bright sun hours earlier.

With the Red Sea to our left and the empty darkness of the Sinai Peninsula to our right, we followed our location on Google Maps and motioned to the driver when to drop us off. Phone flashlights lit our way as we kicked through the sand, following the sounds of the sea. My kids once again joked about my plans, and I hoped we'd find the dreamy beach hut I had booked.

I sighed with relief, seeing multicolored painted rocks lining a path. A woman's welcoming voice filled the darkness, guiding us to a thatched roof hut near the water's edge. Rugs covered the sand with seven mattresses spread out on top. She told us it was perfect weather for pulling the mattresses out and sleeping outside. Excited by a new adventure, we believed her that there was nothing like falling asleep under a canopy of stars next to the Red Sea.

> We may have eaten ramen for dinner, slept on sandy mattresses on the ground, and skipped showers for a few days, but we were rich in time, and I cherished it.

The sound of waves lapping against the shore woke me up. Conked out farther down the beach, Corbett and Hudson weren't budging. With the rising tide, if their beds had been a few feet over, they would have mimicked the scene in *The Parent Trap* when Meredith Blake woke up floating on a mattress. Only on the other side of this water was Saudi Arabia, not a lakeshore. Nothing in my life felt real anymore.

Two women chasing a dream built the camp. With every painted rock and repurposed palm branch, they created a life away from the city's noise. I felt connected to their story of picking a path unconventional to the masses. In planning, I knew our family would need a peaceful place to debrief everything we experienced in Israel; and I booked two nights at the camp. We pulled striped cushions up to short tables under a large hut and feasted on a breakfast of cucumber, egg, tomato, pita, and *ful*, a dish like refried beans with a definite twist. Evann licked her bowl clean.

Following a few mentally and emotionally draining days in Israel, we collapsed in the Bohemian-style paradise. Aside from our hosts, we felt completely alone on the banks of the Red Sea with no Wi-Fi or cell service. Between hours playing Rummikub and walking along the shore, we processed the previous months' experiences and dreamed about what was in store. We may have eaten ramen for dinner, slept on sandy mattresses on the ground, and skipped showers for a few days, but we were rich in time, and I cherished it.

With the girls and I content in hammocks, the guys took off to explore a snorkeling spot down the road that our host recommended. Abandoned resorts lined the route. Dogs howling in the distance highlighted the absence of people. Some resorts were in mid-build, while others looked completed but never opened. At one point, an empty resort's lazy river lined with pool chairs curved past a locked medicine cabinet behind a poolside bar. It was apocalyptic. *What happened here?* my guys wondered while also deciding it made an ideal paintball location.

Our hosts helped us locate a van to drive us south to our next destination. Along the way, we passed the miles of the abandoned resorts. We learned that after a revolution in 2011 and a terrorist attack on a Russian airplane, tourism crashed in Egypt. All construction on the stretch of coast came to a grinding halt. Resorts abandoned by developers now covered land once belonging to the Bedouin community. Disarray dominated the beach. I spent the ride wondering about the communities that lost their land. How long had they been on the shores before developers took over? Where were they now?

Dahab—a Boho Beach Town

World-renowned for scuba diving and kite surfing, Dahab was an eclectic oasis in the shadows of the impressive and imposing Sinai mountains. Once a Bedouin fishing community, the town featured a single main strip lined with open-air cafés with hanging baskets, dive shops with handwritten signs,

and vendors with trinkets. Green palm trees popped against the brown of the landscape, and the super chill town vibe had a definite backpacker feel. It was an invitation for lingering.

The girls and I picked a coffee shop next to the guys' dive shop to park ourselves for the week. We sat at the same table daily, soaking in the sun and consuming too many brownies, thick shakes, and lattes. It was fall in Oklahoma, but our year of summer was going strong.

When we overheard a group of teenagers chatting in English, Evann turned to me and said she had forgotten how it felt to understand what a group of teens was saying. Tourists from Europe and Russia strolled the same quaint main path, but we were the only ones with an American accent. Local shop owners asked us why US citizens didn't visit. We struggled to answer them but affirmed we wished more from our home could experience their home and hospitality.

Nearby, one of the world's deadliest dive sites attracted divers from across the globe. Of course, my guys wanted to learn to dive there. What better place than one with that kind of record? In reality, the location was deadly for those who pushed their skill level and dove to depths that caused oxygen deprivation, leading to disorientation. My guys would not be doing any of that.

For five days, they worked toward their scuba and advanced scuba licenses. The only time their laid-back instructor didn't have a tea in his hand was when he was underwater. He won over my guys with his knowledge, humor, and genuine joy in life. They learned Everett swam the same way he walked, never in a straight line. While gliding among turtles, stingrays, lionfish, and octopus, they joked their dad was slow, always dragging far behind. For Chris, watching from a distance as his sons reveled in something he loved was better than anything else under the surface.

When Everett emerged from the dive center after the final test, he had no idea if he passed but knew he did better than Corbett (which was more important as the younger brother). With passing scores, they selected photos for their licenses. Everett chose one in a suit where he looks like a young James Bond. Hudson opted for a Hawaiian shirt with a fake island background. Corbett picked a selfie with a terrible mustache. Their personalities reflected in their choices, and I hoped they would be forty-year-old men with non-updated scuba license photos one day.

While the guys dove, Breese, Evann, and I became open-air coffee shop regulars. Each afternoon, a young girl with enough English to make sales and hold basic conversation burst into the café with armfuls of bracelets. She asked Evann about the scar on her lip (cleft lip) and wondered if the "holes" on Breese's leg were from a gunshot wound. We used hand motions to explain they were from a broken femur and traction. She lifted her shirt just a bit to reveal a scar on her belly and gasped when I showed her my amputated toe. Horrified that a doctor removed it, she told me he was a "very bad doctor." I laughed and assured her he was an excellent doctor. I appreciated her curiosity, and the slightly offensive way language barriers made her questions come off. Before saying goodbye, she asked me to take a picture of her and Evann making a heart with their hands and told us to remember her.

And I do. I think of her often.

She left me smiling, and with countless questions—did she have ten siblings, as she said? Did the youngest die? How did she get her scars, and what was school like? When people buy her bracelets, where does the money end up? Engaging with kids during our travels was beautifully complicated. They frequently asked hard and personal questions and typically left me wrestling with topics that rarely crossed my mind at home.

> Leaving a town was always bittersweet. Each week, I'd fall in love with a new place, pack my backpack, and head to the next.

On our final morning, I returned to the little café on the water for one last visit. Leaving a town was always bittersweet. Each week, I'd fall in love with a new place, pack my backpack, and head to the next. I knew I'd probably never visit Dahab again, because the world is enormous and I love the unknown. I took my time alone to breathe in the sea air, feel the wind on my face, and sit criss-cross applesauce on my favorite café cushion in the corner.

Cairo—a Cultural and Political Capital

A city like Cairo can be overwhelming if approached with a list of must-see places to squeeze into a few days. We devised a small list of locations to visit and left the rest up for wandering. Corbett needed to replace his computer screen, which had cracked back in Jordan. We spent a day crossing the city chasing down different tech stores and districts based on Google reviews and personal recommendations. The task gave us a unique way to explore parts of the city we would not have visited otherwise.

Dodging people, cars, motorcycles, and buses, we headed toward Khan el-Khalili, Cairo's historic district bazaar. Randomly, we turned down side streets based on what caught our eye. The guys noticed a car stalled out on a busy one-way street. Joining with a host of men, they pushed until it started again. I soaked it in, watching them on that street, laughing and helping. It was what I had wanted for them: the chance to see how similar the world was. Less than a year earlier, we were leaving my mother-in-law's funeral when we noticed a car stalled out on the highway ramp. They had jumped out of our car, still in their funeral clothes, to help push the car to safety. Now they were doing the same in the dizzying city of Cairo.

Cars and people buzzed in every direction. We counted between the sounds of car horns and couldn't make it two seconds. The honking was incessant. Adding to the noise, little boys blew horns as loud as possible. "That would have been me," Hudson said, smirking as he passed. A few feet later, he came across another group of boys with a goal of noisemaking. This time, he joined in, hyping them up, yelling, "*Yallah!* Let's go!" and evoking laughter and high fives. The famous market fascinated me, but the side streets with kids captivated me.

We eventually needed to grab a taxi and could have taken two, but Cairo was chaotic, and I had no desire to navigate it in two vehicles. The driver was willing to squeeze eight in his five-passenger sedan, so we went for it. Chris, Breese, and the driver took the front seat. I piled into the back with the others. Our five bodies layered together. Narrowly missing cars and pedestrians, I whispered, "I don't know how we haven't gotten in a wreck." Approximately two seconds later, we hit a stopped car while going about five miles per hour. Our driver threw open his door, waved his arms wildly, blamed the parked car, and we drove off. Cairo was the only city where we encountered a street I refused to cross on foot.

For our final day in the Middle East, we hopped on the metro, a bus, and a microbus to get to the

Pyramids of Giza. I knew the Pyramids were close to the city and not in the distant desert. However, even knowing that ahead of time, it was astonishing to drive down the street and suddenly see the Pyramids and the Great Sphinx in between dusty apartment buildings. We waved at the bus driver to let us off, and we meandered a few backstreets toward the less common entrance. Passing short palm trees between homes, I looked up at the laundry drying overhead despite the perpetual dust from sand that filled the air. With the Pyramids ahead, we hugged the side of the street as a donkey pulling a rickety orange cart passed us.

Given that the Pyramids are the only remaining of the Seven Wonders of the Ancient World, my mind could not wrap around their age or the history they were the backdrop to era after era. Everett posed for a photo with the socks his friends had given him. He had been capturing images in epic places, and next to the Great Sphinx was an obvious choice. Hudson preferred an angle of him kissing the Sphinx while Breese spun in front of the Pyramids in a long yellow dress. We ended our time by hiking to a ridge that placed the Pyramids between us and the city in the distance, highlighting the contrast between the ancient and the modern.

Before the day ended, we met up with friends for dinner in a bustling, trendy area of town. We feasted on food in a fancy restaurant with tablecloths and servers constantly checking on us—a far cry from our typical dining experiences. At 9:22 p.m., I looked down at my watch between dinner and dessert. "No upcoming events" flashed. *Except boarding a plane to fly to a different continent in a few hours*, I thought. I never imagined I'd be eating dinner and forget that the next day, I'd be on the other side of the world. Our new normal was weird, and I loved it.

WISDOM AND WONDER

Egypt marked our final stop before Southeast Asia. We were beginning the downhill, prompting us to consider home. I spent most of my life in a ten-mile radius. I remember when Target was an open field, and the corner shop on Main Street was Petrik's, where they served burgers and shakes. I know when the toll road went in and how the Bradford pear trees filled the landscape with beauty and the stinkiest smell.

In Dahab, I realized our time away had become a respite—a Sabbath. It had a start but also an end. As time passed, we had space to reflect on what we wanted life to look like when we returned. Fiercely loyal and stable, I had commitments I carried on for decades. Things I led. Ways I volunteered. Relationships I invested in. I wondered how much had become an obligation or by-product of my loyalty over intention and choice.

Then I boarded a plane and walked away from everything. When we returned, I could have a fresh start in a familiar place. As I discovered new countries and asked about differences, I was also asking questions about home. What would I pick back up, and what things had run their course?

Cultural Insights

After exploring the Grand Egyptian Museum, my kids spotted a movie theater showing Black Adam, and we impulsively bought tickets to a showing in English. Halfway through, the lights came on, and everyone walked out. We looked at each other, trying to figure out what was happening. We were the only family, the only nonlocals, and the only ones confused. It was our first experience at a movie with an intermission.

The girls and I stepped into the bathroom and stood next to young women adjusting their headscarves, double-checking their outfits, and reapplying lipstick. Surrounded by young couples on dates, we saw a side of Egyptian culture we would have missed at the popular tourist destinations. We could have done a million things in Cairo, but going to an old theater on a whim was the perfect fit for our family.

Budget Travel: Shift the Funds

A tremendous amount of budget travel involves cutting costs in one area to spend more in another. For instance, at the Pyramids, we used public transportation to get there and opted out of camel rides on the grounds. As a result, we spent about $11 instead of $145 and had extra funds for other things. When the guys picked the Red Sea as the dream spot to get their scuba licenses, we chose to skimp on lodging to put more toward diving. We spent the week at a two-star budget motel with paint buckets next to a wall and bougainvillea over the entrance to our rooms. It was barely a step up from our thatched-roof beach hut, but we had no plans of doing anything but sleeping there.

Your Adventure

When have you been impacted in a positive way by watching someone do something unconventional, and how did it influence you?

INDONESIA

Completely disoriented by my alarm and the total darkness, I stretched out and felt walls on both sides. It was the first time I had no idea where in the literal world we were. And then I remembered. A red-eye flight landed us in Jakarta, where we checked into a hostel and squeezed into a dorm room with eight pod-style beds. My kids, overjoyed not to share beds, embraced the claustrophobic conditions.

After a few short hours of sleep, Chris and I lured them out of their cubbies and jet-lag-induced exhaustion with the promise of baked goods. As we stepped outside and into light rain, the humidity assaulted Evann, who had proclaimed the arid desert her favorite. In stark contrast, I was elated with every puddle my sandal-strapped feet splashed in.

We wove through streets teeming with life and royal blue *tuk-tuks*. Jakarta was our big-city stop in Indonesia, our chance to savor the country beyond the beaches that often fill travel feeds. Southeast Asia is nothing like Oklahoma, but it felt like coming home. I was ridiculously happy. Toward the center of an alley, we found a bakery on a street filled with food stalls, various simmering soups, and plastic buckets brimming with vegetables. We feasted on tiramisu, strawberry shortcakes, and lattes with a cacophony of aromas wafting around us. Breese sighed in pure delight with each bite she took, and Evann declared the donut she munched on to be the first good one she had ever tried. Everything we saw, smelled, heard, and tasted was glorious. We all felt it.

The sugar and caffeine rush energized us to continue for hours of meandering and eating. After months of Mediterranean dishes, Everett craved orange chicken. We could only laugh when he returned from a food court with a plate of chicken feet, a significant detail lost in translation. From *koshari* for dinner in Cairo to chicken feet for lunch in Jakarta, things changed quickly in twenty-four hours.

A Most Thoughtful Lunch

An invitation to a traditional Padang restaurant from online friends highlighted our time in the metro. The food was incredible, but the true gift was the friendship and the chance to share an actual meal instead of digital messages. We devoured little bowls of a variety of foods with curiosity and fun. Watching Evann try cow brain was both shocking and exciting. At some point in our travels, she decided to just go for it and try foods and experiences she typically shied away from. Throughout lunch, I frequently gazed down the long table at my family and our friends in complete awe that we were there together.

As travel-related conversations tend to go, we covered a gamut of topics: the similarities and differences between our cultures, the ease of exploring that comes with a US passport, and what life was like in Indonesia. We shared about our faith, and they gave us more insight into Islam. Lingering at the table, we sipped avocado juice, deeply grateful for their generosity and kindness to our family.

As we began saying goodbye, they gifted us two bags of goodies with a sign that read "Campbells' Indonesian Care Package." Little notes explained each item inside and gave us a glimpse into local food. It was an astonishingly thoughtful way of teaching us new things about a place we already loved. With hugs and a few group pictures, we parted ways and returned to our cubby-hole hostel for a final night in Jakarta. In the morning, we'd hop on a plane to another one of Indonesia's seventeen thousand islands.

Lombok—Kuta Beach

From the airport, the hostel van zoomed past palm trees, cinder block walls, thatched roofs, and food carts covered by umbrellas. Instead of gas stations, wooden stands held rows of glass bottles filled with neon-green gasoline for the sporadic mopeds carrying locals and tourists alike. I was born to live on a tropical island and somehow ended up in landlocked Oklahoma. I am forever grumpy about this displacement and the winter months that come with it.

We pulled into the tropical oasis of our hostel. Evann dropped her backpack in our bungalow and dove into the palm-tree-lined pool. Chris tested the Wi-Fi connection for work while the guys began a game of Monopoly Deal. Breese strolled around like her mom, delighting in the details of her home for two weeks.

Beginner and seasoned surfers returned to the hostel each night and engaged my guys in games of pool. Everett sunk an eight ball while trying to explain to the twentysomethings why he wasn't at home doing school. On a Zoom call, Chris talked loud enough for everyone to know his work agenda. I kept telling him that just because he was across the world didn't mean he had to yell. In a chair by the pool, I wanted to jot a few notes on my phone, but my reading glasses were back in my room. My waning eyesight and Chris's unreasonably loud phone voice reminded me of the vast age gap between us and the other guests. We were ancient among the crowd, and it was past my bedtime.

Late nights led to sleeping in for most of my crew. Savoring the alone time, I started a much-loved morning routine: eating the hostel's fresh banana pancakes and then walking a quarter mile

to a convenience store for a one-dollar iced latte. One of the many things I'd learned while traveling— if I found something good, I had better soak it up because it may not be at the next spot.

We settled into this new town immediately, walking a single path daily and waving at the same shop owners. The guys bought a two-week pass to a gym run by Australians while Breese found another bakery. We ate endless plates of *mie goreng* (stir-fried noodle dish) and *nasi goreng* (stir-fried rice dish). Bandaged backpackers, who overestimated their moped skills, kept pharmacies busy doling out gauze and antibiotic cream. There was no hurry, no rush, no hustle. Corbett decided he found his retirement town.

Hostel Perks

Our hostel offered moped rentals for a couple of dollars a day. After referring to the banged-up guests as examples of what could go wrong, we paired up and piled onto four mopeds and cautioned our guys to be sensible but have fun. We rode through the picturesque countryside with small villages and rice fields dotting our path. Kids ran around homes and darted across streets. To my shock, five school-aged boys shouted, "Boo!" and flipped us off as we rode past. Later, Everett told me we drove through their street soccer game. Oops.

We arrived at a beach known for excellent beginner waves. There were no modern buildings or trendy surf shops, which was another reason we picked its location. Homes made of concrete and bamboo butted up next to each other. We dodged chickens in the narrow alleys, smiled at families eating in courtyards, and laughed with kids surprised to see our large family renting boards.

Keeping up with her brothers and dad, Evann caught waves with the grace and perfect form of a natural. Breese and I took more tumbles than the rest. We supported family-owned businesses and

spent less than fifty dollars on four mopeds, four surfboards, seven meals, an umbrella, and a lounge chair. I could only imagine how expensive the day would have been in a nearby resort area. We did without comfort-oriented amenities, but my kids learned to surf while gaining perspective from those who called the shore home.

Along with cheap moped rentals, the hostel offered us a massive discount on a snorkel tour since it was the rainy season and tourism was quiet. On our way to the sea, one of the guides mentioned seeing a couple of US tourists in town for the big holiday weekend. Chris and I looked at each other. "What holiday?" Pausing to ponder what month it was, we laughed at the realization Thanksgiving was the next day.

An outrigger picked us up and dropped us off among three uninhabited islands for hours of swimming amid the coral and fish. One island held a small snack shack run by three teenage girls. By the time we left, one had written "I love Everett" in the sand, and all three had snapped hundreds of pictures of and with Everett and Hudson. I told Everett to tone down his smolder.

Driving back to our hostel, I was overwhelmed by the beauty of the world and people outside my window. All around the globe, kids played games in fields, moms nursed babies, communities came together for weddings, neighbors shared food, teenagers stayed up too late, and families held each other close. The world was not chaotic, dangerous, and full of despair. The narrative I read was very different. While there was pain, suffering, and hurt, there was still joy, laughing, and hope. So much hope.

Thanksgiving in a Village

Just as our snorkeling guide predicted—Thanksgiving Day arrived. We couldn't create any semblance of our traditional holiday, so we opted not to try. Instead, we embraced the lack of regularity by taking mopeds to visit a village that had existed for fifteen hundred years. A handful of residents offered tours, accepting donations, of course. We connected with an outgoing guide, who had spent years teaching himself English. We were grateful for our chance to learn from him.

We rambled through narrow passages, taking advantage of gaps between homes to admire the palm trees jutting up from green hills and the grassy fields encircling the village. Our guide led us to the home where a midwife had delivered him. Three steps led into the house, signifying the three phases of life: womb, earth, and afterlife. A woman napping inside remained utterly unfazed by our presence.

Our guide explained that the village's homes were communal. Everyone shifted homes based on the community's needs. Large families lived in larger homes; parents switched to a smaller one when kids moved out. Older adults lived in ones without steps. We climbed a tower built during COVID when the village closed itself off to outsiders and monitored anyone approaching. The perch built during isolation delivered a magnificent view in every direction.

The importance of community over self was a thread woven through all our guide shared. Everyone did what they could to support the whole. Fascinated by it all, I asked too many questions. I probed him on what happens when two people have a massive disagreement. He stood silent, then thoughtfully responded, "I am sorry I cannot answer that question." There wasn't that type of conflict. He said siblings, spouses, parents, and kids disagree, but disagreement on an intense scale between village members didn't happen. My face showed my disbelief at his words. "I understand it might seem impossible to you," he responded. It did.

I was keenly aware that I saw only a tiny glimpse of this place nestled among Indonesia's islands, but it felt like a place of belonging. I heard only one man's story, but it caused me to pause and reflect on my community. Traveling the world had become a case

study of my home country, which looked increasingly different with every passport stamp.

We thanked our guide for his hospitality and returned to town for Thanksgiving dinner, splurging at a local restaurant. Chris and I ordered buttermilk chicken sandwiches with aioli and coleslaw. The boys ate loaded burgers, Breese picked a stacked berry waffle, and Evann devoured a breakfast burrito. It was a very delicious, though very untraditional, Thanksgiving dinner. The Instagram-worthy café with palm tree murals and white-painted cinder blocks was a far cry from the simplicity of the village—two places close in physical proximity but worlds apart in most other ways.

After dinner, Corbett ditched us to take a moped and explore—he needed solitude and an adventure alone while the rest of us watched storm clouds form off the beach. The rounded sand grains could easily be mistaken for quinoa. I had never seen or felt sand like it and delighted in the creativity of God, who made even sand in countless different ways.

Pancakes Followed by Dinner

We habitually stopped by a food cart serving souffle pancakes in various flavors like matcha, tiramisu, Nutella, and strawberry. The owner taught himself the culinary skill from TikTok videos. We liked the pancakes but returned nightly for the friendship.

Despite working multiple jobs and having limited time, he and his wife invited us into their home

> Traveling the world had become a case study of my home country, which looked increasingly different with every passport stamp.

for dinner on our final night in town. We navigated the short ride down dusty one-lane roads on mopeds and entered a courtyard surrounded by the homes of his extended family. His mother sat on a concrete porch, bagging ground coffee to sell. She reminded me of my grandma, who often shucked corn on her front-porch glider. Waved into their home, we gathered in a circle on the floor as they brought out bowl after bowl of food. I watched Hudson devour an entire plate of barracuda, the bones piling up and falling off his plate. We never came close to finishing the food as we laughed and built bridges of friendship.

Our time in Indonesia began with an invitation to share a meal surrounding a restaurant table in Jakarta and ended with an invitation to share a meal in a home, circled on the floor of Lombok. To both invitations, our emphatic response was "Yes!"

WISDOM AND WONDER

A constant theme of our travels centered on how people lavish their neighbors, strangers, and friends with kindness. We are a large family. We come with many mouths to feed and take up a chunk of physical space, yet someone invited us to their table in nearly every country we visited. The generosity and goodness of our hosts captivated me. Things often seen as barriers to hospitality, like homes being too messy, too small, or needing more furniture, were not hang-ups to those who made space for us. Sitting at tables or on floors worldwide, I thought of the ways fear frequently sits at the heart of the struggle in welcoming others into our homes and lives— fear of things not going right, fear of being judged, unaccepted, or misunderstood. I didn't want fear robbing me of anything.

Cultural Insights

While we sat at a little café, the daily rain fell through the palm umbrella onto our table. It reminded me Jakarta was sinking and was predicted to be at least partly underwater by 2050. As a result, the government was moving its capital to another Indonesian island about 650 miles away. The whole idea of moving the capital of a country fascinated me. Unbeknownst to us, two islands over, an earthquake was causing schools, homes, and buildings to come crashing down. Most of those killed were children in school, and upon hearing the news, my mind could not wrap around the deep pain and agony of that reality.

Because of its location in the Pacific Ring of Fire, Indonesia's natural disaster rate is one of the highest in the world. Traveling connected us to the places we stayed. World news was not a headline of a random location. It was the stories of the faces and places we had the gift to know. From our rainy lunch, we returned to the hostel to check in on staff and talk with the local business owners we had met. Indonesia was grieving, and we grieved too.

Travel Tip: Find "Our" Place

During our first week in Morocco, we established a family agreement to find a place we love and return to it as much as possible. While there was gain in trying new shops and restaurants, our family found a groove in having at least one place that became "ours." It was our way of making home everywhere we went and getting to know owners and employees. Instead of saying, "Remember the desserts in Indonesia?" we say, "Remember the strawberry shortcake at *our* bakery in Jakarta?" Bakeries, cafés, and food carts dot the world that we now claim as our own.

Your Adventure

What are your biggest hurdles when it comes to hospitality—to welcoming others into your home or community?

MALAYSIA

A choir sang "Silent Night" next to a Christmas tree as Santa approached us with little bags of Yimu cookies. His thick ruby-red velvet robe was a far cry from our shorts and T-shirts. Palm trees swayed outside, and I hadn't worn a hoodie in months. Santa could keep his layers, and I'd keep my tank tops. It was my kind of Christmas weather.

Moments earlier, when we stepped out of the international arrival terminal, I had expected a sea of taxis and Ubers calling for our attention and the ringgits we had just exchanged our dollars for. I was not anticipating entering a mall with passengers pulling luggage and teenagers carrying H&M bags. Evann spotted a Subway and wanted a six-inch ham and cheese. A large sign above the escalator read "Welcome to Malaysia." We hopped on the metro conveniently located inside the mall.

A security guard checked us in, and I pulled back the curtains on the floor-to-ceiling windows to reveal an expansive view of Kuala Lumpur. We went from a hostel with bunk beds, bandaged backpackers, and all-night karaoke to the twentieth floor of a high-rise apartment in one of the fastest-growing cities in Asia. We welcomed the change and the magnificent view. The skyline includes the world's tallest twin towers among miles of creatively designed skyscrapers.

Eating snacks left for them by the host, my kids questioned how the apartment could fit our budget. For fifty dollars a night, we had a rooftop infinity pool, three bedrooms, a kitchen, and a gym, were close to the metro, and had views for days. I loved that my kids could embrace the not-so-clean and gritty places we had stayed, but listening to them squeal at the posh and fancy was sure fun.

From our skyscraper perch, we noticed umbrellas popping up in a narrow street and a market forming underneath them. We headed straight down for dinner. Malaysia has three primary cultures: Malay, Chinese, and Indian. I was determined to experience them all. Passing tables overflowing with ears of corn and pink baskets filled with ombre shades of orange tomatoes, we dodged water puddles in search of dinner. Giant woks sat next to rows of rice cookers and vats of oil. Tables replaced cars in the street, and we jockeyed with residents for one with three small plastic stools. Breese stood in wonder as a man tossed vegetables and meat, called out orders, and flung sauces.

Forgotten Retainer

Getting ready to snuggle into her big fluffy bed, Evann realized she left her retainer at our hostel in Indonesia. After years of dental and orthodontic work related to a cleft lip and palate, we had timed her medical needs with the trip in mind. I panicked at first, wanting to maintain the ground she had gained.

The following day, I searched "Invisalign" and "orthodontist" on Google Maps, hoping for a nearby lead. An office with incredible reviews was located ten minutes away at a mega mall. Chris sent a WhatsApp message at 10:00 a.m., and she had an appointment at 1:00 p.m. By 1:05 p.m., retainer molds were complete, and we ordered McDonald's McFlurries downstairs. Three hours and fifty dollars later, she had an excellent brand-new retainer.

Overwhelmed with how simple, fast, and inexpensive the entire process turned out to be, I tried to imagine a Malaysian family visiting my city and attempting to get a replacement retainer in a day. The paperwork and expense would be overwhelming. We took Corbett back the next day to replace his retainers because they were old, and it was shockingly easy and affordable. Things like custom fitting a retainer in a foreign country often seem complicated until tried. In the previous months, we replaced prescription glasses, a laptop screen, several pairs of shoes, clothes, and a retainer with relative ease in numerous countries.

We walked miles in Kuala Lumpur, experiencing its diverse areas, foods, and cultures. Our lips went numb from the intense spices of *tikka masala* in Brickfields (Little India). Corbett and I could barely breathe from the heat but couldn't stop eating it. "My mouth is on fire!" I said, laughing between bites of garlic *naan* and *masala*. Walking along the red-, orange-, and yellow-painted sidewalks lined with sari shops and curry wafting in the air transported us to a different part of Asia. Decorative arches in various colors provided a barrier between those of us on foot and those in cars. It all made Chris's longing to visit India intensify.

In other areas of town, realistic paintings and abstract art covered surfaces from electrical boxes to buildings. We turned down a narrow path between restaurants and emerged on an empty street with every inch painted. Swipes of green hues carpeted the asphalt like grass. The exterior air-conditioning ducts were caterpillars climbing the building. Birds, flowers, butterflies, and bees covered walls, gutters, steps, and doors. As we soaked in the surroundings, a door opened, and a woman tossed a bucket of water onto the grass-painted street—a reminder that this was not a popular walking street but a back alley to apartments and restaurants. The spectacular mingled with the mundane was a combination that demanded my attention and affection. Art on the streets instantly makes me smile.

Hospitality Delivered and Invited

A DM on Instagram from a woman I had never met welcomed our family to her country. Since she was away and we couldn't meet, she offered to have breakfast delivered. Her thoughtfulness stunned me. A few days later, a driver for a company similar to DoorDash delivered a feast of typical breakfast foods. I spread the white boxes and little baggies of liquids across the table. The woman ordered us dishes we would never have known to try and sent a message explaining each item: *nasi lemak*, *chee cheong fun*, *mie goreng*, kaya butter toast, *roti jala*, and curry chicken. She sent iced Milo, iced coffees, and *teh tarik* for drinks.

I became a quick fan of kaya toast with its slab of butter and caramelized coconut milk. The food was delicious, but it was the act itself that moved me. I had always thought of hospitality as welcoming someone into my home. She showed me that hospitality can look like a breakfast delivery. Though not physically present, she welcomed strangers into her home country and shared a meal with us.

Days later, we gathered around two tables in the home of new friends for another shared breakfast. Hudson entertained the youngest daughter with magic tricks, and all the kids played hide-and-seek. They graciously answered our questions about their family, home, and Malaysia. We shared stories about our travels and life in Oklahoma. Taking a scenic route back to our apartment, they drove us past magnificent views of the city and the mountains surrounding it. Listening as they shared what they loved about their neighborhood, the Kuala Lumpur skyline, and life in Malaysia reminded me of how our Greek host had talked about his love for Athens. It was a gift to love your home and recognize its beauty. As much as our wanderlust called us away, Chris and I chose to bury our roots deep in the red clay soil of home. We, too, loved our home.

Batu Caves—Rainbow Stairs and Perspectives

A 140-foot-tall golden sculpture of Lord Murugan dominated the Batu Cave complex, the most famous Hindu temple outside India. It stood at the base of 272 rainbow steps that led to a temple built inside a limestone cave. Climbing the steps, I avoided being accosted by the dozens of aggressive monkeys while the feisty primates carrying their tiny babies enchanted Evann. Every surface of the complex was carved and painted in shades of pink, green, red, purple, yellow, and gold. I immediately wanted to understand the spiritual significance of colors and design in Hinduism.

As a family, we ventured around the caves and tried to understand the importance of what we saw. I felt deeply grateful for the opportunity to learn about the world's religions through firsthand experiences alongside my kids. The more we learned, the more similarities and differences we understood. Understanding religious beliefs helped us understand worldviews, motivations, priorities, politics, and people.

As we traveled, we asked, "How is our perspective of the world shaped by growing up in the United States and by our faith?" We wondered the same about others. "How has her Hindu faith molded her view of what is important? How has he been shaped by growing up in Egypt?" Observing and interacting with differences compelled us to ask reflective questions of ourselves and others. Standing in a vibrant temple taught as much about home as it did those worshipping on its grounds.

Melaka— a Charming Coastal City

I had no idea what would be waiting for us when we stepped off the bus in Melaka other than a guesthouse with glowing reviews about the sweet couple that hosted. The sidewalk tile changed eight times between the bus stop and the guesthouse. The last country we visited with constantly varying sidewalks and floors was Italy. I never guessed I'd be strolling Malaysia's streets and thinking, *This reminds me of Italy.* Chinese characters painted on round columns supporting two-story buildings guided our path. The Dutch ruled Melaka from 1641 to 1798, which explained the mash-up of Dutch architecture and Chinese lanterns. The town was colorful, unhurried, and the perfect mid-seventies temperature. Green trees fought against concrete to grow and fill in cracks. A monitor lizard popped its head out of the river cutting through town. Murals and bougainvillea bordered the waters, and fiddle-leaf fig trees soared in concrete planters.

Our hosts greeted us enthusiastically and showed us our rooms. She pulled out wrapping paper and asked my kids to decorate empty boxes to place under a Christmas tree. He pointed to a town map painted on the wall and asked us about our interests, ensuring we could fully enjoy his home. They welcomed us each morning and afternoon with a local snack from the market or a homemade baked good, insisting we try everything.

It was the low season, and the quiet streets gave us a different perspective of Malaysia than what we experienced in the bustling capital. In the evenings, themed *tuk-tuks* blared music with neon lights matching the beat. They catered to visiting guests, a large percentage Chinese. Corbett made Breese's dreams come true by riding in the neon-pink Hello Kitty version.

Melaka was founded nearly four hundred years before the United States and was the most important trading port in Southeast Asia during the 1600s. Its history reminded me that I learned only a fraction of world history in school. A lack of knowledge of other lands and cultures can lead to an isolated or skewed view of the world—one that falsely places individual countries in the leading role and the rest of the world as supporting actors.

> A lack of knowledge of other lands and cultures can lead to an isolated or skewed view of the world—one that falsely places individual countries in the leading role and the rest of the world as supporting actors. Travel blows up egocentrism.

Travel blows up egocentrism. When it came time to depart, our hosts hugged us and sent us on with homemade chocolate chip banana bread. I held it close to avoid the ravenous teenagers who would devour it in a minute flat. We missed out on all the Christmas festivities back home but gained a taste of the holiday on a strait off the Indian Ocean.

We reached the halfway point of our trip. Before we left home, I anticipated our travels would unfold at time-lapse speed. The opposite proved true. We had hit the brakes hard in June and then restarted in the very slow lane. Corbett pointed out life no longer seemed to fly by because we could vividly remember something significant from nearly every day, for sure from every week. We packed a tremendous amount of newness into each day. There was no blur of repeat. The change was good. We were good.

Hudson Made Dinner Plans

While in Indonesia, Hudson met a bodybuilder from Malaysia who was in town for a competition. They shared contact information and reconnected at a nearby gym when we arrived (the gym was in the same mall we replaced Evann's retainer). Between lifting sessions, they planned to bring their families together on our final night.

We began the walk toward the restaurant as the clouds moved in, and a sprinkle turned into a downpour. Men selling umbrellas to tourists clamored for our attention. Given that we were already drenched to the bone, an umbrella seemed like a frivolous cost, and we were boarding a plane in the morning. Thankfully, Malaysia has a tropical rainforest climate. We were wet but not cold. We reached the street market and met with Hudson's friend, his wife, and their kids. Gathered around a large, round table, we ate plate after plate of food. Bowls of stingray were continually pushed in Hudson's direction, as his friend reminded him to eat lots of protein to build muscle.

I sat back, enamored with the scene. Chris and I didn't initiate this friendship. We were Hudson's guests, invited to dinner in Malaysia by a friend our son met in Indonesia. I expected many cool experiences and moments to come with traveling with teenagers, but this was not one of them.

At sixteen years old, Hudson had navigated finding gyms in every country and making connections as he traveled. He knew how to book accommodations near public transportation, exchange money, grocery shop, ask for directions, and navigate most unknowns. Most importantly, he made friends easily anywhere. I was confident he could hop on a plane to any place and thrive. His brothers could too.

We concluded our three-country tour of Egypt, Indonesia, and Malaysia at tables filled with new foods and friends. Stuffed and still dripping, we hugged goodbye and parted ways, then looked to the next adventure with gratitude.

WISDOM AND WONDER

We arrived in Malaysia knowing only the locations of our Airbnbs. When I chose the locations, I looked at the 2D Google map and picked spots near a market or metro station. We had yet to learn about Kuala Lumpur's spectacular skyline and didn't know it was a street art oasis. We had no idea Hudson would end up ten minutes from a friend he met in another country or that we could eat *tikka masala* in Little India for lunch and have noodles in Chinatown for dinner.

One of the gifts of traveling with a "show up, wander, say yes to invitations, and soak it in" approach instead of a detailed itinerary or bucket-list lens is that I rarely had any expectations. Unmet expectations in travel can lead to frustration and make the uncomfortable miserable—especially when the expectation is that a place will be like home. Malaysia was very much an "I have no idea what to expect, let's go check it out" destination. Everything grabbed my attention and imagination.

Cultural Insights

Instead of the chaotic crowd we encountered in many countries, an orderly line formed to board the Kuala Lumpur metro. Restaurants brought us glasses filled with ice, a big reminder we were not in Europe. We ate *pad thai*, *tom yum*, fried rice, and chicken glass noodle for fifty cents each—a significant difference in cost from home. Honking was the city soundtrack in Cairo. It took two days before we heard a honk in Kuala Lumpur, a city with an estimated population of 8.6 million. We all noticed. I loved that my kids recognized the differences in how cultures approached life, both in the big elements and in the simple ones, like using a car horn. They were appreciating what they noticed rather than assessing which was right or wrong, lesser or better. I looked forward to the unfolding of their perspectives at home.

Budget Travel:
Plan Ahead Where to Stay

Finding accommodations that would hold a large family and fit our budget required advance planning. The flexibility of last-minute bookings can work well for singles or couples and those not limited by funds. We did not fit into any of those categories. We kept our lodging costs small by booking early, traveling to less popular places, staying outside the tourist hubs, and booking places that were good enough rather than the dreamiest spots. We also only booked accommodations that allowed full refunds in case our plans changed.

Your Adventure

How has your life benefited from a relationship with someone with different beliefs, culture, religions, politics, and so forth from your own?

HUDSON
age sixteen at the start of the trip

Growing up in a family of seven, with parents who possess a wanderlust that knows no bounds, has made my life pretty crazy. Only a few seventeen-year-old Americans have passports, let alone have been to twenty-six countries. I have a pretty good grasp of how uniquely different the various parts of the world are. Even with the constant change of landscapes and cultures, one thing followed us where we went: the importance of community. Take Italy, for instance; meals were not about eating food but about sharing time with people close to you. In Italy, gathering around the table was about sharing laughter and stories. One person in Italy told us you can quickly spot Americans in the crowd. How? He said Americans are the ones who will eat or drink while they walk.

Whether it was the Thais and their games of *sepak takraw* in the park or Filipinos playing basketball, I realized that community isn't just about coming together for special occasions; it's about finding joy in life's simple pleasures, in the company of others. When we went to places like the Tenement basketball court, my mind wondered how people could be so happy living in areas that were so poverty-stricken. Now that I look back, it's because instead of focusing on what they didn't have, they concentrated on what they did have, which was a fantastic community most of the time.

Believe it or not, my mind doesn't think of places when I think of the trip. It remembers people. Whether Ben the Brit, who wanted to ride a camel rodeo style or Alwinn the bodybuilder, who invited my family to dinner, each encounter added a layer of richness to my understanding of the world and my place. As a seventeen-year-old with a passport filled with stamps and a mind full of memories, I've come to appreciate the diversity of communities I've been lucky enough to encounter. Living in a world that often feels so broken and separated, I learned from this trip that community ties people together. Our travels taught me to be grateful for what I have and to slow down occasionally.

Now that I'm back home, I'm learning to appreciate the community around me. While I may not have a park that everyone goes to each night to hang out, I do have other forms of community. Whether it's the late-night Cane's runs or the Wednesday night youth events, being surrounded by community brings joy to life. Abroad, we were told that America is a time-equals-money culture. Who doesn't want to be rich, after all? However, I have now come to realize that true richness is being surrounded by people you love and enjoying life's little moments.

THAILAND

The sky spit rain on us as we bounced in the back of our host's pickup truck and into a junglelike area outside Krabi, Thailand. When he picked us up at the airport, he suggested we get an additional taxi and split up so that no one had to get wet in the back of the truck. However, he didn't yet know us. Chris, Corbett, and Evann jumped in the cab while the rest of us were figuratively and literally soaked in the rain. Being piled in the back of a pickup in an unfamiliar place with my kids makes me giddy. Add a little bit of rain, green mountains, and towering palm trees, and if I had died at that moment, I would've died a happy woman. Eighteen-year-old me dreamed about traveling the world and chasing adventures, but it wasn't time back then. Doing it with Chris and our kids was even sweeter now. Bouncing down back roads in southern Thailand, I knew the younger me would be so proud I didn't let our dreams die. Waiting, working, and imagining for so long made the experience immeasurably richer and any travel challenges lighter.

Red dirt led us to our host's house. His family lived on the bottom floor, and a hammock-filled porch wrapped around our space on the second floor. He introduced us to his rescued gibbon, who was whooping, hollering, and swinging from branches at our approach. After dropping our backpacks

> Bouncing down back roads in southern Thailand, I knew the younger me would be so proud I didn't let our dreams die.

and colorful signs seemed tiny against the towering limestone karsts. Little outdoor restaurants served *pad thai* and fried rice for forty baht, the equivalent of about a dollar. We found a remote-controlled car perfect for the birthday boy at the 7-Eleven. Outside the store, a green *tuk-tuk* was prepared to make deliveries, and I wondered if I could volunteer for the job.

Andaman Sea— More Than Pretty Beaches

A 2004 tsunami devastated the nearby coast and impacted everyone we met. Many locals told stories of loved ones lost and the unfathomable terror of that day. Those who shared their heartache also relayed their love for their home. They served heaping bowlfuls of curry at beach cafés, welcomed travelers to the sparkling shores, and offered tips to reach their favorite secluded beaches. They taught us the ways the water gave and took away.

Borrowing our host's truck, we followed back roads in search of recommended beaches. We parked in a dirt parking lot with a cow munching on grass under palm trees. I'd trade Oklahoma cows for palm trees or move to Thailand and have both. Hiking in the general direction of the water, we took several wrong turns in a forest filled with rubber trees. Liquid latex dripped from metal spouts pierced in the trunks. Little black bowls caught the organic material. Thailand was the world leader in natural rubber production. The process fascinated us and distracted us from the reality that we were lost.

After we finally found a narrow path down a cliff to the shore, miles of empty sand and warm water rewarded us. As we splashed in gentle waves under a brilliant blue sky, my mind replayed the stories of loss written nearly two decades earlier by the tsunami. The memories shared with us changed our perspective of the water. We didn't watch the waves

off, we followed him to a turquoise creek, where we met the resident otters. Our home for the week was a mile from the nearest village and a drive away from town.

The remote retreat came with views of the jungle, the swift creek, and mountains popping up in the distance. Most surprisingly, it also had the fastest Wi-Fi on our trip, according to Corbett, who had been tracking speeds. Our host introduced us to his family and invited us to join the upcoming birthday festivities for his employee's young son.

Needing to find groceries and possibly a present, we walked toward the one-street village. When the quiet road came to a T near a mosque and a school, we took a left and stumbled upon a little drink stand seemingly in the middle of nowhere. We ordered iced green tea with lime, iced coffees, and Italian sodas for a couple of cents each. Pretty pumped that ice was a thing in Thailand, we designated the stand "our place" and returned each day of our stay. Walking back roads came with a close-up view of the community, a benefit not found when flying down the street in a car.

We continued alongside homes and acres of rubber trees while being passed by *tuk-tuks* carrying residents, who were surprised to see our big American family. My heart jumped as we turned down the main stretch. Two-story buildings with faded paint

in fear, but we gained an understanding that caused us to pause and recognize the sacred stories the water held.

Krabi—the World Cup

Our final night in southern Thailand fell on the evening of the 2022 World Cup. As we bounced between countries, we became acutely aware of the international love for soccer. We rented our host's truck to drive to the nearby town of Krabi, hoping to watch the match among a crowd. When we spotted a large pavilion with chairs and a giant screen near the water, we assumed it was for the game. We grabbed dinner from the street market and a few hours later, locals and tourists filled the empty seats.

Everett won a pregame contest for naming all the Asian teams in the World Cup. He may have shown a C-level aptitude for art history while in Italy, but here he earned a solid A+ in sports and geography. The international mix of fans made the setting electric. The crowd erupted when Argentina clinched the title, and my kids flew from their seats, chest-bumping Thai teenagers and shouting in victory. It was our first World Cup, and we were admittedly new fans, but getting caught up in the crowd and excitement was easy.

Bangkok— Christmas in the City

Everything was dark as we left the metro station and walked to our hostel. We stopped in a tiny restaurant along the way for a midnight dinner. The weather was perfect for eating outside, and Christmas music played overhead. When fireworks began exploding in the distance, I looked at my family. It had been months since we left home, but I still couldn't believe what we were doing. I felt profound gratitude for the time with them and the stories we

were writing together. Meanwhile, Corbett found deep joy in the 7-Eleven cheese toastie he had waited months to try.

Chinatown always tops my list of places to explore in a city, and Bangkok held one of the world's largest, with over a million ethnic Chinese. Bangkok's Chinatown, Yaowarat, was established a year before the American Revolutionary War ended. When I think of how much the United States has changed since the end of the war, I can't help but wonder what the streets of Chinatown looked like when the original Chinese population in Thailand built them.

Bougainvillea spilled over balconies, and tables with red Coca-Cola awnings overflowed with oranges. We ate dumplings from street carts, drank iced coffees from a vendor on a backstreet, and meandered through the expansive maze of shopping stalls and neon signs in Chinese characters. While other parts of Bangkok seemed to cater to tourists with modern designs and comforts, Chinatown felt frozen in time. I was enchanted.

The guys found a basketball court near one of the two hundred malls and continued their worldwide court tour. We explored the festive modern districts decked out in Christmas decor and kept our eyes open to what made Bangkok unique. As we did with any big city, we researched which parts to avoid and where not to go at night. We spent a week delighting in the friendly people, vibrant colors, and fascinating history. We'd been to several massive cities and Bangkok was high on our favorites list.

While the guys played endless games of Monopoly at the hostel, the girls and I decorated our dorm room in paper snowflakes. When we decided to keep our cookie-decorating tradition going, Breese and I scoured the neighborhood for supplies only to settle on crackers and frosting. The decorating was a flop but fun. Sprawled out on beanbag chairs, we watched

Elf in the lounge while taking breaks to FaceTime a friend and her newborn son. Christmas looked similar and strange in equal doses.

After a Christmas Eve church service, Chris and I picked up presents for the kids—expensive snacks we usually said no to purchasing. Back at the hostel, we laughed at the realization the red bags I picked for wrapping were hazardous waste bags with skulls and crossbones. Merry Christmas, kids.

We surprised our crew with a Christmas dinner cruise along the Chao Phraya River, a thoughtful gift from a lifelong friend. "Jingle Bells" in English blared from speakers as the boat approached the dock. Wearing our very worn, semi-clean clothes, we clashed against Thai families in stunning holiday outfits. The long buffet table of local and international dishes delighted our senses and stomachs. We cruised past skyscrapers and high-end malls with the words *Gucci*, *Louis Vuitton*, and *Cartier* reflecting off the water.

Breese and Chris joined the emcee on stage to swing dance as "Gangnam Style" played, and the top-deck crowd cheered. I looked around, trying to find someone who found the music and dance combo as oddly funny as I did. Nope, it was just me. Soon, "Silent Night" filled the air as we passed Wat Arun, a Buddhist temple. Christmas looked nothing like the ones I had known.

Chiang Mai— Seconds and Thirds, Please

Hudson realized that if he woke up early and walked a few feet down our street to get me an iced coffee, I'd give him extra baht to buy his own. He did the same in Indonesia. It was a win-win partnership. I sipped my drink while leaning over the guesthouse kitchen balcony to watch the quiet street below wake up. Hundreds of power lines webbed together connected small businesses and homes, potted plants overflowed into the street, and monks gathered plates of

food left for them as offerings. Students climbed into *songthaews* to ride to school.

The guesthouse came with complimentary breakfast each morning and a cat smitten with Evann. I lived my best life waking up to *pad thai*; and Evann lived hers sneaking the cat into our shared room. It was only an issue when she forgot one day and locked it inside, unbeknownst to the owners or us. At lunch, several blocks away, her eyes grew big with panic when she remembered the cat asleep on her bed. We laughed (knowing the owners adored her like she adored their pet), quickly finished our meal, and rushed back to find the cat quietly exploring our room. No harm was done, but no more sneaking the feline into our room. Evann continually reminded us once we returned home that we promised she could get a cat.

Our time in the northern town of Chiang Mai revolved around food, specifically dinner at the street markets. Carts with stockpots that possibly hadn't been cleaned in a decade simmered with broths. Dumplings, spring rolls, mango with sticky rice—we tried nearly everything we saw. We joked with the kids that their stomachs of steel came from drinking out of the water hose and growing up in a family that believed in the five-second rule. Not once had food from a street vendor or hole-in-the-wall shop upset any of our stomachs. Chris pinpointed a *roti* truck he had tried twenty years before in college (one he spent decades telling us about). It may not have lived up to its legendary status, but we still ate the crepe-like dessert every night.

In a dark corner of the market, a woman served up big bowls of *khao soi*. Red curry paste mixed with a thick coconut cream broth and combined with chicken, noodles, scallions, cilantro, and lime created a dish originating in the area. Every night, I returned and ordered the same bowl. I squeezed around a kid-size table on a tiny stool, added more chili, and devoured my bowl, drinking the last drops. I savored the food and setting—different languages, sticky tables, heavenly aromas, laughter, and small lamps lighting up little carts.

When I close my eyes, I remember every detail and physically ache for one more night at that table.

At Last She's Seen the Lights

When New Year's Eve arrived, I asked the guesthouse owner about rumors of lanterns released in celebration. Breese dreamed of living out her own *Tangled* moment and we all wanted to help make it happen. The owner didn't think there would be a release. I joined a local Facebook group and asked there too. No one had a solid answer, but all signs pointed to no lanterns. I prepared Breese for the letdown.

We walked around the historic area of town to join the various celebrations and got foot massages next to a park with live music. A band playing banjos and singing a mash-up of "Take Me Home, Country Roads" and "Oh! Susanna" provided the background music when suddenly a faint light appeared in the sky. A lantern!

It was nearly 11:00 p.m., and we rushed out of the park with Everett in the lead in hopes of making his sister's dreams a reality. After nearly an hour of no luck, a *tuk-tuk* driver appeared and saved the day, allowing seven of us to pile into a space meant for four. He drove through the tiny alleys honking, swerving, and avoiding pedestrians and walls. I couldn't stop laughing. Breese began singing "I See the Light" as the driver narrowly avoided collisions. It was the best kind of total chaos. Either we were going to see the lanterns or we were going to crash trying. Thankfully, he hit the brakes when the alley dead-ended, then he dropped us off in the middle of the fun.

We joined the mass crammed in the narrow street. Lanterns became entangled in trees and power poles. "This is a definite fire hazard," Evann stated. The countdown began, followed by "Happy New Year!" wishes. We watched with grins as more lanterns floated in the sky, accompanied by fireworks and cheers from the crowd. It was everything Breese dreamed it

I couldn't stop laughing. Breese began singing "I See the Light" as the driver narrowly avoided collisions. It was the best kind of total chaos. Either we were going to see the lanterns or we were going to crash trying.

would be. We ended the night by ordering seven Oreo McFlurries and promising to make it a New Year's Eve tradition wherever we were, knowing McDonald's restaurants are easy to find.

Monk Chats

For a week, we watched young and old monks out in the community. We saw the offerings of food left outside homes and the money trees taken for the new year. Chiang Mai is home to three hundred *wats* (temples). A local *wat* offered "Monk Chats" once a week designed to allow young monks time to practice English while also providing tourists insight into what it meant to be a Buddhist monk. Attending a chat became a priority for me.

As we approached outdoor tables at the back of the temple, it looked like a high school was letting out. We often joked that Chris purposefully led us past schools when students were released because extroverted students always spoke up, and he relished the interactions. Sure enough, a group of teenage girls giggled at the sight of Hudson, and one bravely said, "You are really handsome." Watching their brothers squirm at compliments had become regular entertainment for Breese and Evann. We sat down with an eighteen-year-old monk and for forty-five minutes learned about his daily life. He joined my high schoolers in conversations about their favorite subjects in school and shared the challenges of their teen years. He taught us what it looked like for monks to depend on the community to provide their meals and shared lessons in meditation and self-control.

We were surprised to hear he planned to be a monk only for a few years to help pay for his education before pursuing a career as a pilot. I had wrongly assumed that being a monk was a lifelong commitment. There was a big difference between reading about religion and listening to someone across the table share about their faith. Whether in a temple in Thailand or around a table at home, the importance of listening to those with a different perspective was the same.

WISDOM AND WONDER

We spent every evening in Chiang Mai at a large community park near our guesthouse. After several nights watching older men play the local *sepak takraw* game, Hudson asked if he could join their circle. Most were well over seventy years old and could high-kick like a teenage cheerleading squad. They welcomed Hudson in (and later his siblings) with big smiles and encouragement.

Local parks and basketball courts were the gateways for making connections and memories worldwide. The men learned Hudson's name and asked him to return each night. Back in the planning stages of the trip, I didn't know we'd end up in communities with thriving parks where residents of every age gathered each night or that the experiences gained from those long evenings outside with others would be one of the most sacred threads of our travels.

Cultural Insights

On New Year's Day, we heard music from a truck with speakers stacked ten feet in the air. The festivities of New Year's Eve were over, and curiosity pulled us in the direction of the sounds. As we got closer, we noticed money tied to trees loaded into trucks. People gathered at tables, smiled, and waved for us to join them. The trucks full of trees headed to the temple as offerings for the new year. The celebration stood in opposition to what I typically saw on January 1. I was used to parties on the last day of the year, followed by announcements of fasts, cleanses, reading goals, exercise challenges, and other messages aiming to bring about transformation into the best version of oneself. The joy of the local people and how they spent the first day of the year giving and celebrating as a community struck me. A few minutes of observing and being in their presence gave me a refreshing picture of what the beginning of a year can look like.

Travel Tip: Think Through Your Preferences

When we began thinking through where we would be on December 25, I asked the kids if they wanted something quiet and low-key or a big, bustling city. Since Christmas was already nothing like at home, they all voted to embrace the change and spend the holiday in Bangkok. Christmas in Bangkok was the opposite of home, allowing us to celebrate the differences instead of focusing on what we were missing. Every traveler has different preferences, and taking the time to plan accordingly helps ensure more enjoyable experiences.

Your Adventure

Have you ever tried a food culturally unknown to you and immediately loved it? What was it? Where did you try it?

VIETNAM

A tiny plastic table with little blue stools sat empty and beckoned to us. We had yet to learn what the restaurant served, but the nearby tables overflowed with happy Hanoi locals. That was all the sign our growling stomachs needed. In Southeast Asia, we learned that dining spots next to curbs filled with locals almost always meant the food was in our budget and excellent. We asked for a menu, but there was none.

We glanced around and realized the restaurant offered one dish—*bun cha*. It should have been evident to us since it was written all over every wall in bold sans serif font, but we didn't read Vietnamese and thought it was the restaurant's name. Cross-cultural travel is an endless lesson in humility. Crammed around a miniature table under a giant red and yellow sign, we devoured the famous grilled pork and noodle dish thought to have originated in Hanoi. It was another happy accident and proof that walking a new street is the best way to discover the local treasures.

Kumquat trees, colorful lanterns, and red banners decorated the packed streets in preparation for Tết, the Lunar New Year. It felt like walking through the Christmas aisles of a craft store, but this one was on the street, and the artists were creating in their stalls. What a gift the world offers us with endless

> **The trick was stepping into the street and moving with eyes fixed straight ahead. Don't wait. Don't stop. Don't hesitate. The mopeds wove around us as long as we kept a steady gait.**

combinations of scents, sounds, and sights. Hanoi had over six million people; each one must have had a kumquat tree. Piled on the backs of mopeds and sitting at every building entrance, the trees ripe with orange fruit were expressions of a wish for prosperity, happiness, and good luck for the new year.

Over the past months, we reached expert levels at finding food, navigating buses, and crossing chaotic streets. The famed streets of Hanoi had nothing on us as we slowly strolled in front of thousands of mopeds to cross a main street. The trick was stepping into the street and moving with eyes fixed straight ahead. Don't wait. Don't stop. Don't hesitate. The mopeds wove around us as long as we kept a steady gait.

Randomly, we stumbled upon a giant stage next to the Red River. The young crowd and dynamic energy continued to build as we tried to make sense of the event. When a band took to the stage, bodies bounced to the electric beat, and glow sticks pulsed overhead. I added "taking my teenagers to their first rave" to my list of things I didn't see coming.

While my family slept a bit longer, I walked to a little coffee shop a few blocks from our two-star hotel to watch the city wake up. At a table on the sidewalk, I sipped my latte and people-watched alone with my thoughts. Next door to the café, a young woman in her twenties joined her grandpa and his friends for morning coffee. Balanced on little wooden stools, they engaged in loud conversation and laughter. The men sighed each morning when she stood up to leave. I sighed, too, wishing I could join their conversation (more accurately, eavesdrop on them). Instead, I leaned forward on my stool, held the ceramic mug with two hands, and thoroughly delighted in the sights of the street.

A woman balanced on a green bicycle with a tray of strawberries balanced behind her. A bamboo *nón lá* hid her face from the sun. A young woman in a pantsuit rode a blue moped wearing a mask to protect herself from the heavy air pollution. Murals covering a wall across the street told the history of Hanoi. After several days of the same routine, the barista commented she could always spot the Americans because they were the only ones who ordered their coffee takeout and walked while absentmindedly drinking. She told me I broke the stereotype, which I was more than thrilled to do.

Ha Long Bay Fishing Villages

Spread out on a boat with travelers from Germany, Israel, and England, we sailed through towering limestone rocks and past hundreds of floating homes that comprised several fishing villages. Our travel route had crossed the path of countless Germans in

multiple countries. "Traveling is our national pastime," one told me, invoking massive jealousy on my part. Over eighteen hundred islands filled the bay, some of them luscious green and others rocky, but all surrounded by sparkling blue water. Kayaks allowed us to pass through caves and play on the shores as the young Israelis shared stories about growing up in a kibbutz.

A local fisherman welcomed us into his home on the water. After having us all take a few steps back, he pulled up a section of his floor to show us his two two-hundred-pound pet groupers swimming below the wood, contained in a net that stretched the length of the floating residence. I had a crawl space under my house. Crawdads and frogs called it home. Different worlds existed above, below, and in our houses.

I will never live on a home floating in a bay off northern Vietnam with a massive grouper for good luck. The fisherman catching snapper at sea will probably never catch a catfish on Fort Gibson Lake in Oklahoma. Our lives were a far cry from each other, but the water didn't see our differences—it carried the sound of our laughter the same.

Cat Ba Island— Seawalls and Volleyball

Our hostel room windows overlooked a sizeable concrete area next to the harbor. An enormous cat statue stood at the entrance, surrounded by kumquat trees in celebration of Tết and the Year of the Cat. Despite the concrete ground and the inherent risk of playing a game involving kicking a ball near a seawall, kids flooded the area each night to play. Mine, of course, joined in too. When the ball plummeted to the water, Corbett won the cheers of a dozen little guys by diving in and rescuing it. He challenged me as a toddler and still challenges me as an adult. With a grin, he said ridiculous stuff like "Gymnastics isn't a sport," just to rile me up. He regularly spouted off information and stats with such confidence I had to pause to

think, *Is this an actual fact or a "Corbett fact"?* He exasperated me and dove off seawalls to save balls for kids he didn't know. I couldn't love him more.

While in town, we rented mopeds to explore the island. Weaving through the island's mountain passes, we stopped by a little family restaurant on the side of the road for lunch. The owner welcomed us with a huge grin and pulled Chris aside to share a cup of tea and stories. A war veteran, he talked about how his town had changed over the past decades and pointed to a nearby cave that acted as a hospital during the war. He knew we were Americans and understood our dads were the ages of many soldiers who fought. He could have asked us a million questions or said many different things, but he offered tea, his smile, and his welcome instead.

As we drove through communities and wandered around small towns, we noticed volleyball was everywhere in Vietnam. On an evening walk, we spotted a group of adults playing a one-on-three game. Hudson asked if he could join. Quickly, it became a game of five-on-five. My sixteen-year-old American son was playing volleyball with nine Vietnamese women and men in the age range of his grandparents. Soon, the neighborhood came to play—groups of locals and Campbells rotated in with each game. The neighbors played together often, which was evident by how they joked. Just as I was thinking how proud I was of Hudson for using self-control and not spiking the ball, he spiked the ball. They roared with laughter and then told him no more. We traveled without a plan most days, and we did a lot of neighborhood wandering because, time and time again, we learned it's where we wrote our most remarkable stories.

Hội An—the Fete of Tết

Our original plans for Tết involved a boat ride to an island to spend the holiday in a Vietnamese home in a remote fishing village. Weather canceled all boat trips, so we pivoted and booked a homestay run by

the sweetest family. Our host welcomed us with juice and towels folded like animals and invited the guys to join her husband and son at the local soccer field each night.

In my usual manner of observing and eavesdropping, my ears perked up when another guest approached our host with a bouquet. He asked her if she knew what Shabbat was and then mentioned he buys his mom flowers for Shabbat each week. Since he wasn't home, he bought some for her instead. An Israeli traveler. A Vietnamese homestay owner. Shabbat on the Lunar New Year weekend and an American mom witnessing another moment of goodness tucked in a little corner of the world.

In between bike rides through rice fields and eating our weight in *gimbap*, *banh mi*, and Hội An noodles, we explored the streets of the ancient Vietnamese town. Hudson tried octopus tentacles on skewers, and Corbett became obsessed with *cafe sua da*, Vietnamese coffee. Pink flowers cascaded down yellow buildings and mopeds lined the sidewalks. Each time I passed a cart overflowing with eggs, I thought of home. At the time, bird flu caused a significant shortage of eggs in the United States and an accompanying price surge. Meanwhile, eggs were in abundance on the streets of Hội An. Travel constantly highlighted how what was true in one place was not true everywhere.

We rented mopeds to explore the countryside and questioned the strength of a couple wooden bridges as we crossed and stopped for lunch at a café on a remote road. The owner didn't have menus but showed us a live chicken. We wrongly assumed he was asking if we wanted chicken with our noodles when, in fact, he was asking if we wished to eat *that* chicken with our noodles. Breese opted for rice only. It didn't top our list of favorite meals in Vietnam but certainly added to a most memorable day.

Unable to ring in the Lunar New Year in an outlying location, we dove into the crowds of Vietnamese tourists along the river that cut through Hội An. I don't remember hearing any American accents, but tourists abounded. With minutes remaining until midnight, we hopped on a little boat to be on the river. Lanterns floated in the water nearby. Crowds cheered on the banks, fireworks filled the sky, and we beamed on the water.

We left the crowd and wandered the quiet streets with closed shops connected to homes. Residents burned paper offerings on sidewalks and roads. The first action of welcoming the new year was remembering those who had passed. Smiles, celebration, and joy filled the midnight alleys. My perspective of how I usher in a new year was challenged and changed in Thailand and Vietnam.

Hours after we had said, *"Chúc Mừng Năm Mới! Happy New Year!"* to those we passed by, I opened my phone to read about a Lunar New Year shooting in Monterey Park, California. My lens of America was limited to my phone and world news stations—and that lens was heavy. Many Americans messaged me to "Be safe," while many others I met traveling asked, "Aren't you scared living in the United States?" Instead of sitting with friends at home, I sat with new friends asking me about my home. I tried to answer questions about US headlines even though I had the same wonderings.

We ate our way through Southeast Asia. I love to eat. I especially love to eat with people who are also excited about food and dive into the dish before them. I relish lingering at tables and soaking in every last morsel of food and conversation. There is an episode of *Parts Unknown* where Anthony Bourdain sits on a little stool at a street café in Vietnam. He remarks to the camera, "All of the things I need for happiness: Low plastic stool, check. Tiny little plastic table, check. Something delicious in a bowl, check." His words echoed in my head as I toured Vietnam one little plastic stool at a time. The smile couldn't be wiped off my face.

On our final night, Chris looked over at me as I held my bowl with both hands and drank the last drop of broth. "I'm sorry," he said with a grin. I knew exactly what he was referencing. I couldn't stay. He booked our final flight home. I booked our last accommodations. We still had four and a half months of travel, but the end was in sight.

WISDOM AND WONDER

I joked with my kids that I felt like I was living my capstone year as a homeschool mom. We were in a unique season as a family, lingering around tables, eating *pho*, and examining how we defined a good life. The years of foundational learning were behind us, and I was discussing profound philosophical ideas with my nearing-adulthood children next to the South China Sea. The conversations, $2.36 *banh mi* sandwiches, and $0.87 fresh goodness in our bowls were tremendous gifts.

Over the previous seven months, we had sped through countless cultures, each with a different philosophy of what makes a prosperous and happy life. Some expressed it in relation to others (community and relationships), and others related it to self (personal health/work/success). Our travel speed spotlighted the differences in priorities. A culture's definition of a prosperous life established the foundation for everything else. While slurping noodles, we examined how the same was true for our lives.

Cultural Insights

As we cut through the water of Ha Long Bay, several Europeans on the tour with us asked our thoughts on the American War. It took a few minutes of confusion before Chris and I realized that what they knew as the American War we knew as the Vietnam War.

I was born after the war ended, but it was rarely discussed in my history classes. During our month in Vietnam, we dove into studying and talking through the war as a family. My kids' education looked very different from my own. Together, we were learning about world history, forms of governments, and worldviews in profound and life-changing ways, often in the very places those histories were written. Sometimes, as when in Vietnam, the learning took a more personal, somber, and heavy turn. I was grateful for the chance to sit in the heaviness with my family.

Budget Travel: Shift It Around

The priorities related to our accommodations constantly changed. I picked places close to basketball courts for the guys, with a pool for Evann, next to a bakery for Breese, and with great Wi-Fi for Chris's work. In Hội An, I found an Airbnb with a design aesthetic that appealed to me but was a bit over our budget. To make it work, I opted to book us an extra-cheap spot before to make up the difference. I also limited our stay to a few nights instead of our typical seven nights. We stayed in all sorts of places and conditions, some dreamy and some that allowed the dreamy ones to happen.

Your Adventure

How do you define a prosperous and happy life?

THE PHILIPPINES

On our drive from the airport, Everett's eyes widened as we passed basketball court after basketball court. Rims seemed to hang on every building and fence. It was clear the sport reached a new level in the Philippines. I had no idea. Of course, Everett knew, which was one of the reasons the island country was high on his list.

Among the Philippines' seven-thousand-plus islands, we picked four to explore. Hoping to break up a long coastal drive after our flight from Vietnam, I booked us a few nights in a tiny town at an Airbnb with guest reviews that raved about the hosts, the mouth-watering bacon, and the french toast. Crispy bacon is one of my sons' primary love languages, and they hadn't tasted any in months. The breakfast sealed the deal, and I never imagined the ways the little stopover town would draw us in and interrupt our plans.

I Could Live Here

As I strolled along the seawall with four of my kids, a group of teenagers yelled to Corbett, "Are you Hudson's older brother?" We had been in town for only a few hours, most spent in our Airbnb, sleeping off twenty-four-plus hours of travel. I wasn't sure where Hudson was, but I was not surprised they already knew his name. Hudson can enter a new space with confidence, charisma, and humor that puts others at ease. His magnetic personality had opened more doors on this trip than a diplomatic passport could have. My best guess was that he had explored the dusty roads to find a basketball court. By the sounds of it, he also found new friends.

The neighborhood teenage girls instantly spotted Breese and cheerfully shouted, "Hello!" to her, giggling as my guys passed. English was one of the official languages in the Philippines, making initial introductions seamless. The entire town was easily walkable, and everyone had heard of our arrival. By the time night fell, my kids were in the fold like long-lost friends who had just returned home.

A dirt road led to a nearby basketball court surrounded by a rusting green fence, palm trees, and homes with shared walls. The recognizable rhythm of bouncing balls filled the street. We quickly learned that most games were "pay to play." The entrance fee depended on the court, and the winners kept the pesos after the refs took their cut. Kids bought little plastic bags of water, reminiscent of the ones goldfish swim in at the fair. A Wi-Fi machine provided minutes of access to those who inserted a few coins. Players discarded their slides up and down the court, opting to play with bare feet. Staying in neighborhoods opened our eyes to cultural details we would have missed otherwise.

While the guys forged friendships and poured sweat, Breese found her tribe. A group of five teenage girls wrapped their arms around her. She was part of the pack. Throughout our travels, basketball made it easy for my sons to make friends. Breese longed for the same. From a rooftop patio at our Airbnb, Evann and I could hear her singing karaoke Taylor Swift songs on the seawall before skipping down the road to the beach, arms locked with two girls. "Well, we know who the introverts are," Evann said with a grin.

We waved at a group of moms who sat outside each night laughing together. Like the cool ocean breeze that blew down the road, their laughter traveled through the quaint town. One of the moms smiled back at me. "Do you know where the girls are?" I told her they had just finished swimming and were building sandcastles. Another mom piped up, "They're just hanging out!" As I turned to walk away, I smiled. It felt like home. My guys were at the basketball court and moms asked each other if anyone knew where their kids were—everyday-life stuff, only I was halfway across the world from my actual home.

On December 16, 2021, Typhoon Rai (Odette locally) wreaked havoc on the Philippines. It battered the town we were staying in, ravaging homes and leaving residents without water and electricity for weeks. Still grappling with the pandemic, the community endured a double crisis. Unrepaired damage marked the landscape in the same ways cheers filled the faded court in abundance.

While hanging out with us, one teenager casually told us his home was destroyed and not rebuilt. When we asked where he stayed, he replied with a huge smile, "With friends," and was off. Another teen asked us if it was true that people in parts of the United States had to drive hours to reach an ocean. We nodded and told him it took us eight hours. Sadness for us marked his face. "We are very poor here, but we have this," he said as he pointed out to the water. "Every day, we wake up and have this outside our door. I hope you like it here."

Like it here? I thought. *I love it here.*

Aside from the obvious physical signs of damage, I would never have imagined the fresh pain endured by this community. From the way they welcomed us, engaged with each other, and celebrated the gifts around them, it was abundantly apparent they were far wealthier than many of those they would call rich.

Bus Benefits

After canceling our next stop and extending our time in the seaside town, the time to leave arrived. We paid $13.00 to ride a bus and then in the bed of a pickup truck to get to our next hostel. A private van transfer would have cost us $83.30. We'd still travel the same way even if we had endless money. We actively sought ways to remove the distance between our family and residents.

On the bus, I squeezed myself and my backpack next to a man with a live chicken in a bag while the rest of my family squished into other available seats. A young mom in front of me with a toddler on her lap and a sleeping newborn in her arms reminded me of my early years of motherhood and the juggling of kids. The toddler leaned his head out the window to get fresh air. After one too many curves, he turned toward his mom and threw up all over her pants. She sighed, patted his back, and continued snuggling the newborn. There was nothing else she could do. We were all sardines on a hot, sticky day. A few stops later, she gathered her boys and exited. Off the bus and ignoring her clothes, she showed her concern for her son as she grabbed him a water bottle and began caring for his needs. Motherhood looked the same everywhere I went.

Undoubtedly, a private van transfer would have been more comfortable, but the bus followed by a truck gave us a glimpse into life in the area. Not to mention, riding down island roads in the back of a pickup with my kids landed high on my list of favorite ways to spend an hour.

I smiled. It felt like home. My guys were at the basketball court and moms asked each other if anyone knew where their kids were—everyday-life stuff, only I was halfway across the world from my actual home.

Cebu, Negros, Siquijor—Neighboring Islands

In the coming days, we'd take more buses, ferries, and sidecars to explore islands, swing across waterfalls, and log hours on basketball courts. Heavy rains meant electricity often went out, allowing us to finally use the headlamps we had packed. We strolled the beach in the warm showers, and I learned that my iPhone sends me weather notifications in the Philippines just as it does in Oklahoma. Only the alerts were for landslides instead of tornados. Amid downpours, I'd watch my three sons ramble up the quiet Philippine street we called home after buying ice cream from a little shop that stayed open, electricity or not. My sons. I had seen a lot of awe-inspiring things in the last eight months, but this view got me the most. As I watched these brothers laughing, pestering, being together, I grasped the sacred sweetness of those days. Before I knew it, we'd

be home. Driving. Graduations. Jobs. Girlfriends. Sharing them with others again. But not yet.

An ombre sunset of pinks stretched across the ocean on our last night—a gift. Oklahoma has breathtaking sunsets too. So does Croatia, Albania, Jordan, Indonesia—and worldwide, the list goes on. I've always had a hard time with what many call gifts or blessings from God mainly because those terms are often used to refer to material possessions or things accessible only to the world's wealthiest. If it can't be applied in a sense to everyone, I wrestle with it. It's a complex topic for me, marked by decades of pondering and observing. However, sitting on this beach, the blessing of the sunset was given to all of us. The couple to my right staying at the fancy resort, my daughters playing in the water, the fishermen to my left worried the tide might pull out their boat, and the little boy rescuing items from the trash to build sandcastles—we all paused and soaked in the painting in the sky—a beautiful reflection of the Creator.

Manila—the Tenement

Basketball became our Philippine theme. When planning for a year away, I asked each kid what they'd like to do or see. Everett's main request was to play basketball as often and in as many places as possible. Looking for courts led us to local places and experiences we would never have known to search out. Since these courts were designed for the community rather than visitors, conversations on the sidelines led to other recommendations and an "insider scoop" on the area. When he heard we'd be in Manila, Everett asked if we could visit the Tenement. I had no idea what he was talking about, but he rarely asked for anything, so I prioritized it.

The Fort Bonifacio Tenement was a public housing block built in the 1960s and home to about three thousand people living in seven hundred apartments (approximately 390 square feet in size).

Seven stories of concrete apartments surrounded a central basketball court, serving as a community hub. In 2010, the government deemed the entire complex unsafe and began the unsuccessful process of evicting residents. Iconic murals on the court drew international attention to the plight of the residents and sparked visits from NBA stars. In December 2022, the International Basketball Federation (FIBA) survey named the court "the best basketball court in the world."

Unsure the guys would be allowed to play, we slowly passed the gate and entered the court. Immediately, three teenagers stopped their game, smiled, and waved my guys into a game of three-on-three. I watched as the six laughed, guarded, and took their shots. The Tenement did not have running water or elevators. Next to the court, residents pulled carts of water from the bottom-level filling station up ramps to various levels. Authorities believed the area was due for another massive earthquake and warned of a deadly collapse of the layers of concrete, but families stayed. I wondered about the residents' options. Did they remain because they didn't have anywhere to go? Did they stick around for the community? Did they stay because they'd rather risk dying here than move? I heard it was all three.

There was no denying the strong sense of community—at least from a visitor's perspective. A church, little stores, a barbershop, a salon, and apartments circled the basketball court. There was also crumbling concrete, clothes drying in the wind, and potted plants lining every floor. A man selling ice cream made rounds and rang a bell a little louder when close to kids. The constant bouncing of a basketball echoed on the walls.

Young kids gave us a tour of the roof with Kobe Bryant murals, pigeons, and a few dogs basking in the sun. Teenagers engaged us in conversation, and adults told us they were glad we visited. We bought snacks from a few shops, and Everett attempted to get a haircut, but the barber was closed. My guys wanted to visit another famous court. I wanted to come to listen and learn.

We walked a couple blocks over and gathered around two little tables on a side street for lunch. We discussed the value of community and the impact of natural disasters as we ate chicken and fries. We talked about worldwide water access, our water usage, and the influential impact artists can make in conflicts between the government and the people. In 2023, the Manila metropolitan area ranked as having the world's sixth-most populous urban area, above New York City, Cairo, Mexico City, and Beijing. All the travel guides told us to stay away; there was nothing of value to gain in the city, so head to the beaches. I'm grateful we planned our itinerary based on what Everett knew rather than the guides.

Baguio—a Mountain Town

Baguio, with its high elevation and lack of coastline, gave us a different perspective of the Philippines than what we gained on the coast and in the capital. The pine trees almost made me forget I was on a tropical island. We arrived in town with zero plans or expectations, which was our approach everywhere. However, Panagbenga, the Baguio Flower Festival, kicked off during our stay, and strawberry farms were a short jeepney ride away. Breese had a minor addiction to the berries, and what could be better than a flower festival? We knew all we needed to know.

Designed by the American architect and city planner Daniel Hudson Burnham in 1904, Burnham Park was the hub and heart of the town. The festival drew masses of visitors and a flurry of activity to the park and surrounding streets. Vendor booths, dance performances, parades, food trucks, and concerts invited crowds to gather throughout the day. Little boats in the shapes of swans glided across a central pond.

With rice bowls and *shawarma* in hand, we settled in at the park to play *sepak takraw* and soak up the details. A little girl in Mickey Mouse clothes drank a Coca-Cola while kicking a Hello Kitty ball. A young mom blew bubbles to her daughter while her dad recorded with his cell phone. A group of college students ate noodles from little paper bowls with red-and-white stripes. Sunlight shone through Hudson's curls. A man with a metal stool connected to his cane made laps as a couple nearby ate mango slices with sugar and chili flakes on top. It was a warm culture nestled in cool mountain air. Sitting in the grass, I let my mind drift to the words of Louis Armstrong's "What a Wonderful World"—a perfect soundtrack selection for all I was seeing and feeling.

> Sitting in the grass, I let my mind drift to the words of Louis Armstrong's "What a Wonderful World"—a perfect soundtrack selection for all I was seeing and feeling.

The islands were unparalleled in natural beauty, but my family remembered the people more than the beaches. From their big smiles on the basketball court to their laughter-filled all-night karaoke, those we met had a playfulness and joy that seemed to set them apart from any others we encountered. Every night felt like a party. It was loud, lively, and the best kinds of fun. Juxtaposed against the enthusiasm was the reality that the Philippines has one of the highest rates of natural disasters. We witnessed the lingering effects of different catastrophes on every island we visited—and yet nowhere else had we experienced such extroverted and high-spirited communities.

WISDOM AND WONDER

In the first town we stayed, I sat at the court watching my guys play and imagined living next door. At one point, I counted fifty-two people in or around the court. Almost all were teenage boys and young-adult men. Ten were playing. The rest were watching, laughing, and shouting at the players. Not a single person was on their phone—those were tucked in bags and pockets. I daydreamed about making chocolate chip cookies for the players (though they'd probably prefer *tortas*) and chatting with moms on the seawall each evening. We had been to many places where I thought, *I could live here*. However, the little town on the coast was the first place I truly pictured making a home.

Cultural Insights

When researching possible countries to visit, I found countless references to Indonesia and the Philippines being the same—pointing to food as the main difference. From the moment we landed, the Philippines felt different, not just from Indonesia but from all of Southeast Asia. It reminded us more of Latin America than the countries sharing the same waters. I'm guessing those who called Indonesia and the Philippines the same probably spent most of their time on the beaches or in the water. They may share similar topography and waters, but they are beautifully unique and equally warrant experiencing.

Travel Tip: Mix It Up

To get a more complete picture of a country, it is important to mix up the destinations. If a tourist came to the US and only visited Oklahoma or the Grand Canyon, the resulting perspective of the United States would be skewed. By including a variety of destinations, like a small town, a suburb, and a capital, visitors gain a more balanced perspective of the country.

Your Adventure

Is your calendar so full that you're missing out on fun with others? How could you create more margin in your life for community and impromptu connections?

JAPAN

The midnight streets were silent, almost as eerily quiet as the Mars-like landscape we experienced in Jordan's Wadi Rum. The setting was different from what I expected for Tokyo. We had exited the subway station, and our first glimpse of our new neighborhood was the glow of a 7-Eleven on the corner of two one-way streets. Back home, most convenience stores functioned as gas stations too. In Southeast Asia, gas pumps were rare—a reminder of the differences in populations that don't rely on private vehicles. Starving and excited to try the famed egg sandwich, we beelined across the street. Chris and the kids went inside to pick out food. I stood on the corner with our seven backpacks in a pile, adding layers to fight the chilly air.

Soon, a young woman came down the sidewalk and stood on the corner in front of me. The light was red. I watched as she patiently waited for the green pedestrian light to flash in the middle of the night. I could have crossed the narrow road with one giant leap. She remained motionless, though no vehicles were seen or heard. Once the light turned green, she walked across.

A few minutes later, a man approached the empty intersection, respectfully stood still, and waited for the light. The entire process was mind-blowing for me. In my community, jaywalking was more normal than using a pedestrian crossing. Many Americans prided themselves on believing that rules were meant to be broken, speed limits were suggestions, and not getting caught was the goal. After only five minutes on the streets of Tokyo, I was enthralled by all I could learn from a culture incredibly different from my own.

Japan was not originally part of our plan. However, Chris found cheap tickets to take us from Tokyo to LA, where we'd connect for our South American leg. I fought him a bit on the route because the weather would be cold, and we packed for summer. However, like always, the budget won. My preconceived notions of Japan were based on movies or random things I heard, all of which were incomplete—if not terrible—information sources.

Chris and the kids eventually joined me on the corner with bags full of yummy treats, and we wandered the neighborhood trying to find our Airbnb. I told Chris I'd handle the cold weather without complaining, but he had to follow all the rules without complaining. It would be equally challenging for us both. There was a part of his soul that died while waiting for a pedestrian light on a street with no cars. I felt the need to tiptoe down the sidewalks and told the kids not to talk—not even a whisper. Stealth was not an attribute our family possessed. Not only were the streets hushed, but everything was pristine and orderly.

The Outskirts of Tokyo

Crisp morning air greeted us as we stepped outside. The neighborhood street consisted of homes butted up next to each other along tiny roads with a handful of single-lot parks and quaint shops mixed in between. Despite the day being in full swing, the chirping of birds and pounding of our feet were the only sounds. Though a train station was nearby, we decided to walk several stops away to soak in the area at the pace of a stroll instead of the speed of a train. At the end of our street, I noticed a small broom attached to a community sign with a dustpan nearby, ready for anyone to use. The concept of a neatly stored broom for residents to work together to keep their street clean baffled me. A few houses over, a Ferrari parked in a driveway caught Corbett's eyes. Very opposite sights grabbed our attention.

As we neared the main road, residents on bikes surpassed the small number of vehicles. A royal-blue trash truck with perfect paint pulled up next to us. It was tiny and looked like it had rolled off the factory line moments earlier. How can a trash truck have a spotless exterior? It was a rolling oxymoron. Passing a construction site, we noticed a sound monitor ensuring the construction site remained below a certain decibel. As a bright teal cement truck also with impeccable paint slowly cruised by, my curiosity fired. Everything around me was neat, tidy, and orderly. And much, much smaller than the US versions. Nothing screamed for attention, yet each area held uniqueness.

Noticing the smooth ground surface and lack of even a tiny hole in the asphalt, Corbett commented, "Whoever is in charge of Tokyo streets should be president of the United States." Oklahoma potholes could easily swallow a cute Japanese truck. Like Corbett, I scanned the path we walked. I recorded the street below not in appreciation of intricate tile as in Rome but in sheer wonder at how it was so immaculately clean. Thousands of commuters passed through the area each day, yet I saw no speck of trash or even a gum wrapper tossed aside. The roads were more sanitary than the tables we had been eating on.

The last time I experienced a cultural shift so surprising that it caused my head to spin was on the

beach in Italy after leaving Morocco. The noticeably calm and peaceful atmosphere reminded us of the Slovenian countryside. A metropolis and a European countryside made for a surprising comparison. After months of karaoke on the streets until the wee hours of the morning and covering our heads with pillows to sleep in other parts of Southeast Asia, we scratched our heads at the differences. Not better, not worse—just so, so different. I was thrilled that my kids had experienced enough of the world that they thought of Slovenia when they walked the streets of Tokyo. My personality lit up around the organization and tidiness while my introverted side appreciated the serenity and quietness.

Connected to the metro station, we peered into the bicycle parking garage. There were rows and rows, levels and levels of bikes. As we watched residents check their bikes into the garage before jumping on the metro, I was struck by how many would be considered well past retirement age in the United States. Their agility, speed, and strength were an inspiring image of what health could look like later in life.

After figuring out train stops and timetables, we made it on the right track and rode silently on a tranquil train filled with residents heading to work. The heart of downtown Tokyo buzzed with life; the buzz was more like a gentle bee than a loud, obnoxious hum. We occasionally noticed a discarded cup on the ground as we reached streets with more tourists. I could only imagine how frustrating it must be for residents to pass by trash discarded by guests.

We made our way to the famed Shibuya Scramble, a massive pedestrian crossing frequently featured in movies set in Japan. The intersection closed to vehicles every few minutes, allowing roughly twenty-five hundred pedestrians to cross in multiple directions. The sheer order of it was mind-boggling. We crossed repeatedly to immerse ourselves in the polite crowd and dizzying experience. We logged miles across the megacity from

> We logged miles across the megacity from temples and electronic stores to districts filled with boutiques, anime, pop culture, traditional crafts, and temples. It was futuristic and traditional, appealing to all seven of us in different and unique ways. We were dazzled.

temples and electronic stores to districts filled with boutiques, anime, pop culture, traditional crafts, and temples. It was futuristic and traditional, appealing to all seven of us in different and unique ways. We were dazzled.

A Convenience-Store Diet

Our shoestring budget did not work for a full foodie tour of Tokyo, which we all felt was a massive loss. It also prevented us from going wild at the vending machines that lined streets and stores. Machines offered salads, pressed juices, desserts, toys, hundreds of drinks, and other specialty items. Prompted by one of Hudson's friends, we hunted down one that offered "cake in a can," a dessert with layers of cake, cream, and strawberries in a clear soda can. It was both excellent and adorable.

Thankfully, Japan had the corner on convenience stores, which made eating on a budget possible for our large family. The stores offered countless fresh and made-to-order dishes and seasonal items. Knowing my access was limited to five days, I ate a 7-Eleven egg sandwich daily. They were the perfect combination of fluffy egg and soft bread. On the way to the counter with my sandwich, I often added a Japanese fruit sandwich made of custard, whipped cream, and strawberries or *ichigo daifuku*, a soft and chewy mochi stuffed with strawberries and sweet red bean jam. Typically, Breese and I shared every strawberry and cream combination, but sometimes we ordered our own.

Eating while walking is taboo in Japan; many convenience stores provide the necessary items for preparing food, like kettles, microwaves, and toasters. Second-story seating presented views of the streets below, bustling with pedestrians and the occasional Lamborghini. We gathered our custom ramen, sandwiches, and desserts, then watched what felt like a movie outside the windows.

Toilet Tourists

The guys searched for and found a court to log another country on their worldwide basketball tour. No longer in the Philippines, they didn't have to pay to play, but they did have to join a queue and wait. Evann, Breese, and I had watched plenty of basketball and decided to ditch the court to explore the surrounding district. One of Breese's friends told her about a restroom with smart-glass translucent walls that turned opaque. It was nearby, so we decided to hunt it down and stop by a park with cherry blossoms in bloom. We'd catch up with the guys somewhere later.

We saw the freestanding bathrooms on the park's outskirts and off a quiet road. The building was translucent from a distance, providing a clear view of the spotless individual restrooms. Once a guest was inside and locked the door, the whole structure became opaque, hiding patrons from those outside. It was wild. We went inside together, closed the door, and laughed while embracing being full-on tourists in a new place.

Japanese toilets were in a league of their own. There were more buttons on the toilets in public parks than in all our cars back home combined. We could control the seat's temperature, the bidet's water pressure, music, drying options, and dozens of other features. Of course, all the buttons were in Japanese, and the only way to figure out what they did was by pressing them. We were ridiculous in our delight and only semi-embarrassed when the three of us walked out to a stoic man passing by our grins and laughter.

When Breese was a toddler, we called her a "toilet tourist" because, without fail, she needed to use the bathroom if we were in a new place. We decided that the next time we visit Japan, we would embrace that nickname and tour more of the impeccably clean and futuristic bathrooms.

Daikoku—Trusting an Online Stranger

When we added Tokyo to the itinerary, Corbett began researching how to visit the Daikoku Car Meet, an icon of Japanese and international car culture. With access restrictions, the only way to visit was through a private driver and vehicle. We told Corbett that if he could find out how to get there and get back, we would be excited for him to go.

Most things can be figured out with a little effort, patience, and creativity. Our kids grew up watching Chris and me approach life with the belief that we don't need to know exactly how things will unfold; we'd figure them out as we went. They saw this mindset work for us. They also saw when it didn't work. Whether at home or in an unfamiliar country, we avoided doing things for them but instead encouraged them to problem-solve on their own first. Mistakes were not a big deal, and we had their backs. Always.

Through digging on Instagram and online, Corbett found a Croatian driver who could take three passengers in his personal car. Hudson and Chris joined Corbett, while Everett kindly volunteered to stay with me and the girls. The guys met their driver at the nearby metro station and were off for the night posing with Supras, Skylines, S2000s, Imprezas, MR2s, Ferrari F50s, and Lamborghini Aventadors among pulsating subwoofers (all those words are like a different language to me). They also learned about Japan from the perspective of a Croatian who called it home.

Corbett's experience was what it felt like for me to see art in Rome. So much of our trip had been random finds and figuring out ways to do stuff. He contacted a stranger on the internet and experienced a world-renowned car meet, but he also learned problem-solving skills on an international level. As parents, Chris and I found it incredibly cool to watch.

On our final morning, we stopped by a bakery on our way to the metro. The shop was tiny, so we placed our backpacks in an orderly pile outside while we went inside to pick out breakfast. Pans and baskets of pastries and baked goods lined the small shop. Customers walked around with tongs, adding items to trays to purchase at the counter. I watched a woman realign chocolate-mousse cream puffs after she removed one, making sure the platter looked pretty for the next person. Next to the cream puffs was a tray of rolls in the shape of Anpanman. Kids recognized the Japanese superhero as one who protects people, honor, justice, and safety. He taught a message of giving of oneself to help others.

With a tray of goodies, we gathered around a sidewalk table. A toaster and cleaning supplies rested on a narrow shelf beside us. I watched as customers took ownership of their messes and left the tables and toaster area pristine just as they found them. I was acutely aware that, as with every place we visited, there was much about Japanese culture, history, and motivations I didn't understand. Regardless, I was moved, inspired, and challenged by the ways I witnessed the display of honor and respect toward others and surroundings during our short visit. I initially balked at the idea of a few days in Japan, thinking it to be too cold and too expensive. I was proved wrong, and my only regret was our time was far too short.

After nine months of being away from the United States, we boarded an American Airlines plane headed for Colombia with a stopover in LA and a promise of Chick-fil-A for lunch. As Evann approached the plane, the flight attendant warned her, "Careful, honey. That step is a doozy." Giggling at the word choice and southern accent, Evann turned to me and said, "I forgot what American personalities are like."

WISDOM AND WONDER

The unexpectedness of Tokyo reminded me why I love traveling to new places and why I like not knowing a lot before I arrive. It was thrilling to wander with fresh eyes and experience the unfamiliar first-hand. When I saw pictures of the busiest streets of Tokyo, they looked chaotic and loud. Based on those appearances, I falsely assumed it would also be dirty and that the crowds would be shoving or pushing to get past each other. Walking its streets revealed an entirely different city than the one I imagined. Though filled with people, flashing signs, gigantic stores, and a Godzilla on a few rooftops, the city had crowds that moved harmoniously, with respect for those around them. It was strangely calm and a feast for all my senses. Tokyo surprised me in the most beautiful ways and reminded me never to form judgments or beliefs about a place I've never visited. It also provided me a new phrase when I need my kids to talk extra quietly in public spaces: "Use your Japan voice."

Cultural Insights

Our Airbnb host left us a note to take a small bag while we explored because trash cans would not be available on the streets. We would need to carry our trash. At the time, it was an odd instruction.

However, walking the city streets, we were shocked at the absence of trash cans. We carried our trash home like we would hiking a beautiful trail. I was fascinated by personal responsibility and respect for people, places, and things in the culture. Though there was much I didn't understand, I could still learn from what I observed, which was that an entire population could respect a massive city. Most US outdoor enthusiasts embraced the idea of "leave no trace" when in nature. In Japan, the same value marked urban areas too.

Travel Tip: Go for a Walk

In every new location, our first action was to take a walk. A stroll around the area provides a better sense of the community. Go without a plan. Pick a street and head down it. If you see something interesting, turn in that direction. Stop at a bakery. Sit in a park. Pause in front of an old door. Make a day out of wandering and letting a place teach you about itself.

Your Adventure

When have you been happily surprised by a country, town, venue, or even a person? How did you feel when your assumptions were proved wrong?

CORBETT
age eighteen at the start of the trip

My entire life, I've known about the crazy dream my parents had to travel the world, but it didn't seem crazy. I was used to my parents making sacrifices for it; many things that would seem weird to others were normal for us growing up. We didn't eat at restaurants, we drove pre-owned cars, and my mom only shopped at Aldi because Walmart was expensive. Watching them prepare for the trip made me also make sacrifices, often without even realizing it. I decided not to date anyone before the trip, because I didn't want to have to navigate that while traveling. I threw myself into work before we left since I could not work while traveling. I fought to be intentional with my friendships since distance would make those relationships hard. Despite preparing, though, I was caught off guard by how isolating the trip felt.

After we said our goodbyes and were a couple of weeks into traveling in Morocco, I ended up deleting/deactivating social media. As someone who rarely gets FOMO, I found it hard to watch my friends hang out over the summer, when beforehand everyone was busy with work or school. Funnily, I got over my FOMO when they went to college, and I got iced coffee and chatted about Buddhism with monks in Thailand. No longer feeling like I was missing out, I reactivated my social media.

Philomath means a lover of learning, and this has described my life for a long time. I didn't experience culture shock while we traveled. Sure, some things were different, strange, and uncomfortable, but I loved the new knowledge. In Oklahoma, my options to discuss topics with those of different views were severely limited, but abroad, the possibilities were endless. I debated religious viewpoints with Muslim friends in caves and tea shops across the Middle East, discussed gun control with a female Israeli soldier whose relationship with guns was defined by the grim reality of death, and shared prayers with a displaced Venezuelan ice cream salesman in Colombia, who only had a hope of seeking asylum in the United States.

Coming home, I was originally frustrated with the few questions my friends would ask. They seemed to care just about a handful of topics because they felt like they saw my trip through social media, but in reality, they saw only the very few things I decided to post online. In many ways, that made the trip all the sweeter, knowing the only ones who knew and could share those stories with me were my family and those who asked about it.

My travels subtly transformed my life. Since we have been back, as a real estate agent, I have met many clients who have had family in places we visited, and I have found great joy in talking with them through a lens I would never have otherwise seen. There is so much culture and diversity abroad, but there is just as much living in your hometown. Sometimes, you just need to look for it. You never know what you may be missing out on.

COLOMBIA

Tired from crossing an ocean but energized by a new continent, we ditched our backpacks at the Airbnb and went in search of dinner. Just past a large mural of the words "God Is Love," Everett spotted a man on the sidewalk with a grill. Next to him, a large yellow "*AREPAS RELLENAS*" sign invited customers. None of us knew what *arepas* were, but they smelled delicious and looked like fluffy quesadillas with chicken and cheese. We ordered two to try. We instantly ordered eight more. I had always dreamed of wandering the colorful streets of Colombia. I should have been dreaming of the food too.

Bogotá—the Streets Were Talking

Knowing our time in Bogotá was short and our understanding of the city nonexistent, I signed us up for a free walking tour focused on how graffiti spoke to the cultural, historical, and political themes in Colombia and Bogotá specifically. We followed our guide through the streets of the older districts of town. "Bogotá is an open-air gallery. Many Colombians don't have access to art. Street art changes that," our guide said as we wandered past murals telling beautiful, complicated, and devastating stories.

Art has served as a nonviolent weapon around the world for generations. It portrays thoughts, emotions, and realities in a way words cannot. I witnessed repeatedly the decisive role it played in changing the course of world history. Colombia was on an upswing after years of unrest. The combination of hope and heartache reminded me of Mostar, Bosnia and Herzegovina.

After taking side streets, we approached a busy intersection where our guide paused us in front of a stunning mural of three people. I grimaced a little when I saw someone had taken spray paint and written over one face. As I began making quick judgments, our guide explained we were standing on a corner where government protests took place in 2019. The mural was a visual memorial for an eighteen-year-old killed during the protests. Over time, the mural began to lose meaning—people (like me) didn't know its history and saw it only as a pretty portrait. In response, words painted across his face declared what had happened and returned intention to the art. Its purpose couldn't be misunderstood by those who could read the words.

I often think back to that wall as a reminder of how quickly I made assumptions about something I didn't know or understand. I can't write a whole story when I know only one character. Travel, like art, teaches me the importance of being quiet and listening first. I quickly learned Colombia was a country battling all kinds of misinformation and false beliefs from those outside its borders.

Our tour guide mentioned many local artists viewed themselves as writers. Their words covered the city walls, amplified voices, cried out against injustice, marked history, and celebrated culture. They also elicited deeply varied responses. Walking around Bogotá, it was undeniable that the streets were talking.

The Coffee Axis

From bustling Bogotá, we trekked to the coffee axis, a mountainous green region producing most of Colombia's coffee. Our time coincided with Everett's birthday and the week his teammates played at the nationals. Knowing it could be a hard week for him to be away, I booked us an apartment with a basketball court on the fifteenth-floor roof. Our host surprised Everett with a basketball-shaped birthday cake, and decent Wi-Fi which allowed for live streaming of the games. Connecting to his dad's hotspot, he even watched the finals while bouncing on the back row of a bus.

The girls held out on their big adventure when the guys went scuba diving in the Red Sea. Instead, they opted for paragliding over the jaw-dropping landscape of Colombia. I was more than happy to tag along. An unstable climb up the mountain in the back of a jeep made us love the adventure even more. While the guides connected the girls to harnesses, Chris and I discussed what order we should go in. We decided it would be best if I went first to be on the ground waiting for Evann. As I turned to tell the girls the plan, Evann ran past, already attached to her guide, ready to fly. She was airborne. No warning. No "Bye, Mom. I love you!" She bolted and took to the sky.

For a long season of her life, *fearful* and *timid* were words others used to describe her. It would have been easy to forever define her with those labels. Riddled with debilitating anxiety related to food after numerous cleft-lip- and cleft-palate-related surgeries, she was five before she ate solid foods. It would be another several years before she felt comfortable enough to leave my side. It took time, patience, and encouragement from us, and significant effort on her part to push past her fears. With each month of travel, she stepped more confidently into unknown scenarios and meals featuring foods so unfamiliar many adults I knew wouldn't have had the bravery to try them. She no longer needed me to have all the answers. Watching her was one of the many highlights of our trip. At eleven years old, she had sandboarded in the Sahara, tried endless international dishes, camped on the Red Sea, surfed in Indonesia, and paraglided in Colombia. *Fearful* and

timid no longer described her. I went from being her cheerleader to simply trying to keep up.

Salento—Hiking Trails and Common Ground

We booked several nights at an old coffee-*finca*-turned-Airbnb in the tiny town of Salento, one of a couple in the region that inspired the setting for Disney's movie *Encanto*. Men on horseback shared the one-way streets with pedestrians, motorcycles, and a handful of cars. Flowers poured from windows, and cafés kept guests caffeinated with heavenly local coffee. Doors and trim on every building were painted a different bold color. Breese danced in front of every door, and I promised she could paint her room's door in a similar way when we returned home. Far from trends and what was popular among her peers, she was developing an eclectic international style with funky pants and bracelets from each country stacked up her arms. I wanted to keep encouraging her self-confidence at home.

In the evenings, a woman rolled a cart to the town square and served *tinto* in little plastic cups from a large bucket. The sweet, watered-down coffee lured Breese and Chris each night. We found a tiny *arepa* shop on the outskirts where the guys and Evann could order five *empanadas* for less than two dollars. Breese and I feasted on *arepas con pollo y queso*, a pan-fried cornmeal tortilla stuffed with chicken and cheese. It became our place for the week—delicious food at a budget traveler's price. The owner smiled when she saw us coming down the lane each day and laughed "*¡Hasta mañana!* See you tomorrow!" when we left.

We piled in a Willys Jeep with a solo traveler from the United States in his midthirties to get to the nearby Cocora Valley, which boasted the world's tallest palm trees. Hudson and Corbett scored the best seats as they hung off the back bumper. The Willys dropped us off, and the fellow traveler walked with us to the trailhead. I was confident he'd soon speed up to ditch our large, loud family. To my surprise, he spent the entire six-hour hike with us. He reminded Evann of Will Ferrell and taught her to rate dad jokes by how many eye rolls they elicit. Amid the ongoing terrible humor, we'd pause in awe of the palms that seemed like skyscrapers in the valley. They could grow to approximately the size of a twenty-story building and thrived in the high-altitude setting.

A heavy mist settled over us as we crossed bridges and passed waterfalls. We told our new friend about the *arepa* shop we frequented and invited him to join us for dinner. Shocked we hadn't worn him out, I grinned as I listened to him swap travel stories with my kids like they were peers. In a sense, they were.

I deeply loved the common ground we found with other travelers. Instead of asking, "Why do you want to go there?" or "Is it safe?" the members of this club would say things like "You're going to love it! The people are incredible!" or "I haven't been there, but it's on my list too!" I knew I'd miss it.

Cartagena— a Party for the Senses

We spent our first few days crossing a bridge from our Airbnb on the outskirts to the colorful historical areas of town. When we first stepped into the arts district, I let out an audible gasp. My eyes feasted on the murals, buntings, lively people, and stunning architecture. The smell of *empanadas* and the steady beats of music filled the air. Monkeys, sloths, and iguanas chilled at the park. I knew I was experiencing only the surface; Colombia was complex, but I was enamored. By this point, my family had learned that it would be an automatic detour if I spotted a street with flags or umbrellas overhead. No questions asked, we would shift course. I took them on a lot of detours. Why would anyone pass up an opportunity to walk under a party?

On a side street, we made friends with a lemonade vendor. Each day, we'd find his cart, and he'd fill big ol' cups for us from a container that looked like a fish aquarium, squeezing extra lime on top. On our second day, he started charging us for five instead of seven. His wide smile greeted us and made us feel like long-lost friends. The people of Cartagena made the city feel like sunshine.

Knowing Cartagena had a history that, as an adult, I barely understood, I signed us up for another free walking tour to learn from someone far more knowledgeable. The tour began with our guide teaching us about Simon Bolivar, who was celebrated by many as the man who led six nations in Latin America to independence. He challenged the group to learn Simon's full name, noting that there would be a test at the end. In a large group, we wandered down cobblestone roads wide enough for only one car. With our return home on the horizon, my heart ached, knowing my days of walking beautiful alleys with handcrafted details would soon end.

I gawked at the colonial architecture. Though Spanish-influenced, much of it reminded me of Rome. I remembered seeing Roman ruins on a hillside outside Fez, Morocco, and Dutch buildings in Jakarta. Jumping from country to country provided an eye-opening perspective of colonization and the stretch of different empires. We stopped in front of a magnificent white church with greenery cascading out of planters lining its front steps. Our guide began telling stories of women killed during the Inquisition in the place we now stood. "Brutal killings," he said. Then he did a 180-degree turn: "But not anymore. Look at how beautiful this street is now. Do you see the bougainvillea?"

Indeed, the bougainvillea trailing down the building was spectacular, but the sudden change of topics was jolting. It didn't matter what town, country, or part of the world I found myself in—including my own—beautiful streets could have ugly pasts. The opposite was true too—ugly streets could have beautiful pasts. I was only passing through and meandered with the eyes of a guest. I saw a Cartagena that was vibrant and

> Instead of asking, "Why do you want to go there?" or "Is it safe?" the members of this club would say things like "You're going to love it! The people are incredible!" or "I haven't been there, but it's on my list too!"

awake; strolling its streets, I felt the same.

Hudson spent the tour learning Bolivar's full name: Simón José Antonio de la Santísima Trinidad Bolívar Palacios Ponte y Blanco. The guide never gave the quiz, but Hudson locked it in his memory. I'm holding out hope that I'll be on his team in a trivia game one day and the random fact will help us clinch victory. Our opponents will think I'm an excellent homeschool mom.

Santa Marta—Unmuted Joy

Tourists by day, but retreating from the bustle at night, we spent our evenings at a neighborhood park. Kids arrived as the sun fell past the court and the shade descended. Basketball and soccer games began with the youngest crowd. Eventually, older teens and adults rotated in and out with each win or loss.

Seasoned pros at being the new kids, my crew jumped in. They'd rather play than watch, so they ditched hesitation a few continents earlier. In every country, we were welcomed in with smiles. I had watched more games over the last year than there were days on the calendar. They had taken place on faded courts, alongside oceans, beside mountains, in cities, and in the countryside. The most valuable possessions in Everett's backpack were a basketball and a pump. They didn't need to know the language; they only needed a ball.

Girls rollerblading made loops on the red track that circled the fenced-in court. They dodged a dog on a leash, pulling a boy on a bike. A few teenagers challenged Corbett to a rapping battle. Across the street, a restaurant with a soccer game on the street-facing TV attracted men on motorcycles. They stopped on the side of the road to check the score and cheer for their team. A melody from a nearby church choir practice added to the cacophony of sounds.

Balls continuously flew into the street. Cars, motorcycles, and adults dodged the balls and gently tossed them back to those playing. No one was upset, short, or rude. Instead, everyone smiled at kids being kids and balls doing what they were designed to do—fly and bounce. A woman my age passed me as she made laps on the track. "*Bienvenidos,*" she said, smiling. I'm a homebody in the US; it was surprising how at home I felt in so many other places.

Nightly, we walked the dirt road back to our Airbnb and passed a little stand selling *empanadas*—a perfect post-basketball snack. We bought out the vendor's supply each night. The apartment didn't have hot water, so showers were quick. As we'd crawl into bed, the neighbors would blast their music and begin family parties. Summer heat and no AC meant the cold showers weren't too bad, but we also had to sleep with open windows. As in Istanbul, I piled all my clothes on my head, trying to drown out the music that beat until the wee hours of the morning. Colombia and Japan had very different views on the appropriate levels of sound. Nothing in Colombia was muted. It was a lively, bright culture full of expression and celebration. We decided if the Philippines had a cousin, it would be Colombia.

WISDOM AND WONDER

We spent five weeks exploring Colombia and staying on the outskirts of towns. When we showed up in a neighborhood, confusion immediately set in at the sight of our big family. I lost count of how often we had been asked, "Why did you want to stay here?" As is common in most countries, travelers to Colombia typically stick to tourist areas, only venturing beyond for work, to offer humanitarian aid, or for a faith-based service. Our presence was a surprise. When we responded by listing the beautiful things we noticed in a neighborhood—the food we tried, the local bakery we revisited, the *sapo* game we learned to play—delight spilled across faces. We saw and experienced the good they knew to be true of their community.

We played basketball on neighborhood courts in little towns because I wanted my kids to realize so much of the world didn't need to be changed. It needed to be celebrated. It didn't need to be feared, it needed to be experienced. Instead of focusing on changing the world or raising world changers, I wondered what it would look like if the goal was to find ways to experience the world (even from our homes) and change our view of it instead.

Cultural Insights

The Andes towered behind the town square, wax palm trees soared above us, and a Spider-Man inflatable with the word *¡Bienvenido!* welcomed kids to come jump. Across the way, a man pulled a wagon with a speaker telling the Sunday night crowd they could buy the local beer. Chris said it reminded him of the guys at baseball games who yell, "Ice-cold beer! Get your ice-cold beer!" My kids were drinking fresh mango-strawberry smoothies while a little guy in a button-up shirt and a fedora flew around the square in a red jeep, remote-controlled by his dad. Nearby, a woman pushed a cart filled with fresh strawberries and grapes.

We found a town square in the center of nearly every town we visited in Colombia, often with a church on one end and a fountain in the middle. Cafés and restaurants lined the other three sides. Quiet in the morning, they functioned as a community hub in the evenings. They were our favorite place to people-watch and one of the many pieces of Colombia we wished we could take home.

Budget Travel: Check Out Hostel Classes

Many hostels offer tours and classes to guests and nonguests alike. In our travels, hostels helped us find cooking and art classes as well as excursions like snorkeling trips. In Colombia, we walked past a beach hostel with a chalkboard advertising a salsa dancing class. For a couple of dollars, the seven of us had a private class with an incredible local instructor and confirmed Hudson was the best dancer among us. Whether you are staying at a hostel or not, check out what nearby hostels offer.

Your Adventure

Is there something you've wanted to do, but it seems too far out of the budget? How might you modify the "how" in order to make it happen?

ECUADOR

Gray clouds hung low, covering the tops of the green Andes Mountains. Our jackets were too thin to keep us warm or dry against the cold air and damp mist as we rode in a truck bed. Hudson's curls bounced with the bumps of the muddy road, and a look of sheer delight covered his face. Eventually, the tires spun, and the only way up was on foot. Our climb ended at a two-story cinder block church. Kids and adults surrounded by sheep began waving as we approached.

The church worked alongside Compassion International to provide basic needs for children up and down the mountain. For fourteen years, our family partnered with Compassion through their child sponsorship program. While in Ecuador, we spent time with one of our sponsored kids and took advantage of seeing the partnership in the remote village.

The women wore rain boots, fedoras, woven pencil skirts, and colorful tops. Their elegance captivated me. At five feet, one inch, I'm typically the shortest in the room. In Ecuador, the average female height is five feet, one-half inch tall. Looking into the eyes of the women around me instead of looking up was a welcomed change. We found it fascinating to notice the physical differences of an area's local people as we ventured through various continents and countries. My guys realized that their "short" stature was relative to living in the US. There were plenty of places where being five feet, six inches was considered tall.

Running between the women, little guys in gray sweatsuits clamored for Everett's attention and the soccer ball he carried. Without delay, they were kicking the ball with my sons, and I was hoping it didn't fly down the slope. Concerned that the high altitude might make us sick, the adults welcomed us with plastic water bottles filled with hot herbal tea. Moved by their thoughtfulness and hospitality, I held mine with both hands and smiled at the women, who returned the expression. Our eyes spoke of the sorrow we felt being separated by a language.

The two-story church was the only nonhome structure in the community and functioned as a gathering place. There was no town. Grassy roads with deep tire ruts connected homes spread out along the sloped side of the mountain.

I thought of the fifty-plus people who chose to partner with Compassion in this region and invest their resources into the lives of the children in the community. Those sponsors may never make it to the little mountainside village and see the kids' smiles shining despite challenging circumstances, but I did. In a time when the news said there wasn't much hope, I continually witnessed the opposite.

Hospitality and Hard Things

A twenty-four-year-old woman and her ten-year-old brother invited us to visit their nearby home. We trekked up a hill through fog and sludge, which made a sucking sound with each step, to the cinder block home their parents had built thirteen years prior. Four years after it was built, and when the younger brother was only a year old, their mom passed away. She left behind a grieving husband and five kids. I was gutted thinking of his loss as I looked into his brown eyes. We stood outside their front door next to the sheep and guinea pigs as they shared the challenges of living in such a remote location and enduring tremendous loss as children.

The young woman worked fifteen-hour days in surrounding fields earning a day's wages equivalent to the cost of a grande latte at Starbucks. She spoke with poise and confidence and reminded me of the many recent college grads I knew who were ready to take on the world. However, in her world, there didn't seem to be a way out of the cycle and the heavy burdens she carried. Her little brother was sponsored through Compassion, which gave her hope for his future. With sorrow etched across her brow, she acknowledged her father was all they had left and asked us to pray for his health. She worried about him as he worked long hours far from home.

It was a bittersweet day, filled equally with beauty and ache. My kids stood on her dirt floor and listened to her words as rain trickled inside the home. They watched their mom hug a little boy who never knew his. Then they went outside and kicked a ball around with him.

Since they were young, we have opted to expose our kids to complex realities in age-appropriate ways. Hard conversations about difficult topics were as much a part of our kitchen as Aldi-brand honey oat cereal. We hoped our kids would grow to be caring and empathetic adults who used their gifts, talents, and resources to care for their neighbors, both near and far, and who would not be indifferent to the plight of others. We played soccer, ate *cuy*, sang, and danced with young children in an isolated village. I watched Hudson take his rain jacket off—the one he searched high and low to find before our trip—and wrap it around the shoulders of a young man. With gifted alpaca sweaters keeping them warm, my kids climbed back into a truck and returned down the mountain carrying a fuller picture of the world and their place in it.

Braving the Amazon

While researching for this leg of our trip, I found a rustic cabin on the edge of the Amazon rainforest

and jumped at the chance to book a week for my family. We arrived by bus, crossed three bridges (one with monkeys), and walked a gravel road to the little cabin. After dropping off our backpacks, I googled, "Are there jaguars in Ecuador?" I'm not a "safety first" person (or second or third), but I figured it would be good to know if we needed to watch for large predator cats while hiking dirt paths. It turned out we didn't.

An old airport runway converted into a spectacular park and numerous courts pulsed with kids and teenagers. When a group of girls saw us approach with a basketball, they immediately waved to my kids to play. It was the first town where an equal number of guys and girls occupied every court. I knew coed games existed in public spaces in plenty of cities, but it was a very noticeable difference after ten months of travel. Watching my crew block shots on the court, I commented to a local man about the number of girls playing. He responded, "Amazon women are a different kind of strong and tough." Whether or not that was true, I didn't know. Nonetheless, they made my daughters feel at home when they aggressively fought for the ball too.

We took advantage of our proximity to the rainforest by hiring a truck and guide to take us farther into the jungle. The kids and I hopped into the back with seven inflatable tubes tied together with netting while Chris, the social extrovert in our marriage, took his usual seat in the cab and chatted with the driver. I avoided passenger seat conversations at all costs, preferring to soak up the scenery of the drive lost in my head. Knowing we'd soon be back home with paved roads and filled calendars, I felt my heart ache. I grieved the end of our year before it was even over.

In the jungle, our local guide pointed to a nest of termites. Hudson followed his lead, smashing the bugs and rubbing the remains on his arms and legs. "The best mosquito repellant," the guide said. We learned about life in the jungle and how to make chocolate and *chicha* (a fermented drink made of

yuca). Returning the favor of teaching new things, Hudson demonstrated to a chocolate farmer how to hypnotize a chicken, a skill he learned on YouTube when we started raising chickens at home.

A long, narrow boat zoomed us along the river. After being assured it was too cold for anacondas and piranhas, I joined the others on the rope swing into the frigid current. Our guide tossed our tubes to float downstream for lunch. I kept my eyes peeled in case a rogue cold-water-loving anaconda wanted to eat me. As we were spread out and floating on tubes in the Amazon rain, I reveled in our reality and wondered if my kids grasped the absurdity of our day. Thankfully, nothing ate me.

Baños de Agua Santa— the Town, Not the Bathroom

A massive change in climate and scenery welcomed us as we journeyed south from the rainforest and into the mountains. Our itinerary was to wander around, shop at farmers' markets, buy a lot of strawberries, and eat all the Ecuadorian chocolate I could find. With five weeks of travel left, I decided to book us one last big adventure—canyoneering. I read online reviews of guide companies and location options, and most mentioned two canyons. One was recommended for first timers, which was us, and provided a fun introduction to the sport. The other was the "do not miss" location for those who relished adventure and a bit of risk. Easy choice. I found a trusted company offering the second option, signed us up, and didn't read any more details. When the kids asked what we were doing, I responded, "I'm really not sure, but it sounds awesome!"

Our tour group consisted of a young couple from England and us. I asked them their thoughts about King Charles, whose coronation was taking place that day. We met countless young travelers from the United Kingdom, and I was fascinated by their varied perspectives and opinions of the monarchy. As we approached the canyon, the guides pointed out large waterfalls and let us know we'd be jumping off them. With questioning faces my kids looked my direction. *I probably should have researched more*, I thought. I responded with a shoulder shrug and a smirk. In a parking lot, we ran through a few quick drills on how to use the equipment, and then there was no turning back. Breese pulled her wet suit tight before a guide dropped her into the first pool of water to acclimate, gasping at the shockingly cold temperature.

The second jump of the day was from the tallest waterfall. The pool below was small and the water was powerful; after my jump, I waited below for Evann to follow me. Looking up at her tiny figure on the ledge, I wondered what to do if she couldn't jump. How would I get back up? She typically needed to know all the details before she made a bold move. And in my lack of research, I provided her with none. I had thrust her into a day of big unknowns, but she had changed on this trip. I saw it more each day. Without hesitation, she launched herself off and plummeted into the pool below. Her head popped out of the water, elated and beaming. She did it; we were both so ridiculously in awe of her.

We spent several hours jumping from waterfalls, rappelling, and zip-lining down the canyon. Rain turned from a sprinkle to a pour, and the guides pushed us to move faster as the current increased and rocks became slippery. A million things could have gone wrong, and there were countless spots where we could have walked away really banged up. It could have ended in disaster, but so could a quick drive to the grocery store at home. Instead...it was one of our most treasured days together. In a nearby roadside café we huddled around warm soup, shared stories, and unanimously decided canyoneering was the perfect final adventure for an epic year. I asked Evann what she was thinking when she stood on top of the tallest waterfall. "I decided to YOLO it."

The guides commented that my kids were fearless. I know them well; none were fearless, but each was brave. Some were more cautious than others. Some

> The guides commented that my kids were fearless. I know them well; none were fearless, but each was brave.

needed more time to think before acting. Some had faced and overcome massive fears. They jumped off waterfalls and went for risky things, not because it wasn't scary but because they learned to process fear healthily. Experience showed them that sometimes what they wanted most was on the other side of fear, not in the absence of it.

Chris and I welcomed risk, unease, the unknown, and the chance for things to turn out awful because of the good what-ifs. What if it works? What if it turns out better than we could imagine? We didn't take it for granted that we were both calculated risk-takers, and the similarity kept us on the same page for most decisions. There had been only one time on the trip that someone probably needed stitches, and it was me. I took a leap and busted my knee. However, it was worth it. I walked away with a scar and a story. I did ruin my favorite pair of pants though.

Back from canyoneering, we stopped by a market for a traditional lunch of soup, grilled meat, rice, beans, fried potatoes, and vegetables. After a few minutes, a young family of three joined us. They looked in their early twenties and had a daughter, maybe three years old. Through broken Spanish, English, and Google Translate, we learned they were originally from Venezuela and were struggling to build a new life. They walked through tremendous trauma and yet smiled with hope.

We shared spaces with refugees and immigrants in almost every country we visited. Sometimes it was an apartment building or street. Other times, it was a dinner table, bus, or taxi. Their profound impact on our family would be difficult to measure. I imagined I'd see the ripple effects of those interactions for the rest of my life. I knew there was beauty in trendy spaces and pristine dining rooms, but was drawn in by plastic tables on sidewalks, where the price of a meal reached a larger demographic. At those tables we gained glimpses into someone else's life in ways that changed ours.

The world was not on fire or innately dangerous and unsafe. Devastating events happened across the globe, even in some of the very cities we visited. However, instability and chaos in one place did not mean they marked every place. In little communities and big cities, we experienced a world of thoughtful and hospitable people, communities looking out for each other, cultures celebrating their history and art, farmers' markets overflowing with produce, groups of kids running around with bare feet and big grins, parks filled with neighbors caring for one another. People worldwide were laughing, giving, and welcoming strangers and friends alike. Our family spent a year bearing witness to endearing people, captivating diversity, and the sacred ways the created reflected the Creator.

WISDOM AND WONDER

Wess Stafford, president emeritus of Compassion International, taught, "The opposite of poverty isn't wealth; the opposite of poverty is enough." After our family heard his words from Compassion staff, we talked about how, in the United States, we often felt a push to acquire more or attain greater success. The latest trend. A bigger home. A newer car. More stuff. As a culture we worked ourselves to physical sickness and relational deprivation in the pursuit of more. It was a rare experience to see someone celebrate contentment. When everyone chased more, abundance was hard to recognize. I wanted to be ever mindful of the point where my *enough* ended and my *plenty* began. Chris and I were grateful for the chance to walk alongside our kids as they grappled to learn the same.

Cultural Insights

The Andean mountain range runs through Ecuador. In addition to the mountains, the Amazon rainforest, Galapagos Archipelago, and Pacific Ocean coast create unique regions in the small country. Based on its size, Ecuador is the most biodiverse country in the world. In 2008, it became the first country to give mountains, rivers, forests, air, and islands the legal rights and the constitutional protection to "exist, flourish, evolve." My family was well acquainted with the concept of constitutional rights and protections. However, extending protection to nature and animals was entirely new.

Family Travel:
Empower Kids with the Cash

In January 2000, Ecuador began using the US dollar as the official currency. By the time we arrived in the country, it had been ten months since my kids used dollars. They learned to quickly convert currency in their heads when shopping for groceries, buying snacks, and paying for their random purchases. In each new place, their first question was "What is the exchange rate?" mainly because they needed to know if the soft serve at the street market would be an easy yes from me. Beyond those skills, they gained the confidence to know they could travel anywhere in the world and buy anything on their own.

Your Adventure

If you could pick any country to visit for the sole purpose of discovering why it is unique, what country would you choose and why?

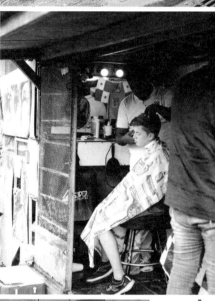

PANAMA

Looking out the plane's window, it felt like we were hovering above a game of Battleship. Massive cargo freighters filled with containers dotted the blue water, waiting for their turn to pass through the Panama Canal. The view was one of a kind. Panama was our last country, and we aimed to begin shifting our focus from the external to the internal by reflecting on the year and preparing for home.

Panama City—Seeking Local Hangouts

Unfortunately, I didn't realize the Airbnb I booked in Panama City was at the top of a hill surrounded by gated neighborhoods. We had grown accustomed to parks, promenades, and town squares where people gathered to relax, play, and end the day together. In those spaces, residents welcomed us to play basketball and get to know them, making our year of travel rich and meaningful. Bakeries, basketball, and buses were the unsung heroes of our travels.

At our new apartment, instead of being immersed in the neighborhood, we were isolated from it. We walked the hilly street each day to head into the city to explore, but each night, we'd return to our rooms on a quiet street lined with tall fences; everyone parked in their garages and shut their gates. After not visiting a similar setting in a year, it was jolting. I understood there could be multiple reasons

In the evenings, we remembered each country and talked about what we learned, the highlights, and the lows. My kids called it our "group therapy" session. I called it being intentional to end the trip well.

a treasure hunt, and the back of minimarkets was where X marked the spot.

With our return home quickly approaching, we took advantage of time in the city to check off a few tasks we didn't want to do immediately upon our return home. Everett stopped by a barber stall under a Panamanian highway for a haircut. His first cut on the trip was in Bosnia and Herzegovina. The second was in Malaysia. Barbershops and salons presented engaging exposure to culture. We began replacing stretched-out and stained clothes, bought a bunch of hammocks, and made online orders for stuff like shampoo to be waiting on us.

Gulf of Parita— Reflecting on the Beach

A few hours south of the city by bus, a fifteenth-floor apartment with breathtaking sea views granted us an ideal place to disconnect and debrief our year. We didn't see another guest in the building or on the beach, which was strange and delightful. Before we left home, I knew it wouldn't be the unfamiliar that tripped up my family, but more likely, it would be returning to the familiar. Seeing other worldviews, ways of life, and cultures with different priorities would mark us. After my college trip to Kazakhstan, I didn't have anyone to help me process what I had experienced, and it felt lonely. I struggled to make peace with a new perspective of my home. I had grown since college, but I was still the girl who learned to be mindful of the statement "I need" when it really should be "I want," and "I don't have time" when it should be "This isn't a priority I have chosen."

Part of me wanted to shelter my kids from the struggles, loneliness, and awkwardness I frequently felt in conversations when my experiences and viewpoints were far different from those I sat with. However, the more significant part of me was grateful for the perspectives they gained and the chance to walk

for gates and fences and knew many had wonderful communities within their walls, but as visitors, we profoundly felt a sense of loss.

We wandered the restored district of Casco Antiguo in awe of the architecture of the buildings that had welcomed presidents and world leaders for decades. Arched windows and bougainvillea dripping over balconies created corridors of picturesque, quaint streets. Tourists snapped selfies in front of pristine churches while stylish restaurants enticed customers with fusion menus and pricey coffee.

A few blocks over, kids played in the street, graffiti marked the walls, and a bottle of Sprite was fifty cents as opposed to three dollars. Instead of tourists rambling the paths, friendly neighbors waved in our direction and greeted us with smiles. We followed a few to the back of a minimarket, where we found a food counter with freshly made lunch for a quarter of the price of the trendy restaurants. Chinese women running the counter shouted orders and shoved coins into apron pockets. Discovering what the average citizen did in a community felt like

alongside them as they wrestled with the challenges that would come.

During the day, we played volleyball on a net Hudson built out of seaweed and tree branches. In the evenings, we remembered each country and talked about what we learned, the highlights, and the lows. My kids called it our "group therapy" session. I called it being intentional to end the trip well. We made lists of our favorite beaches, basketball courts, bakeries, street markets, and bus rides. We talked about the hard aspects of returning, what we looked forward to, what we wished we could avoid, and how we wanted to ban the question "What was your favorite country?" How could we ever pick?

On Being from the States

As we bumped shoulders with some of the many US citizens living in Panama, our debriefing included processing a changing outlook of home and what it meant to be from the United States. Over the year, phones and world news stations provided a limited view of our country in the same ways US news often portrays other places—dangerous, volatile, and unsafe. Clickbait and sensationalism-dominated headlines told a narrative of US implosion over different beliefs, perspectives, and political stances. Our country looked riddled with hate and anger. When I was home, my view was balanced by daily interactions with people, just as when I travel. Smiles from neighbors walking down the street, strangers helping others at the grocery store, and friends delivering meals in hard seasons reminded me daily of decent and thoughtful people doing life and caring for others.

During our year of travel, we also became acutely aware of the privileges that came with our citizenship. Passing through scores of countries with multiple levels of security and procedures, we learned firsthand the ease that came with a US passport. At the start of the trip, we took that luxury for granted.

However, our view changed drastically after standing in lines next to travelers who had a million hurdles to jump at the same border checks we walked through. It was painfully humbling (and embarrassing when it felt like cutting in line). Add traveling with five kids to the mix, and most border agents waved us on through. "Oh, you're American? With kids? Come on through." We recognized the value of our passports and the responsibility we felt to steward them well.

Back in Cairo, we got mixed up in a crowd of students leaving school. A little boy yelled from an overcrowded van, "I love American people!" Several students smiled and wanted pictures, shouting and whispering, "Hello." We also visited towns where faces dropped when they heard we were from the United States. Soberly, we listened as they shared ways our politics negatively impacted their families and communities. I can't name a single policy of another country that has had a difficult and direct impact on my day-to-day life. It was eye-opening. Foreign policy was no longer an abstract idea for our family. International news became tangible as we experienced the ways the policies and politics of the United States affected people around the globe. We wrestled with the global impact of our voices and our votes.

With each country came endless lessons in humility as we attempted to learn a few words and communicate. We had a newfound respect and admiration for those new to the United States who were trying to navigate learning a different language. Speaking a language as a learner requires tremendous bravery and willingness to make mistakes. Chris was the bravest among us. I solidly stood in last place. Going home, we wanted to tackle learning a new language and proactively look out for those in our community who might need extra help, because time and again, we had experienced gracious residents coming to our aid when the language barrier was too great.

Let's Throw a Party

Our final stay in Panama was in a quaint beach house on the ocean next to our host's home. "You guys lucked out. Every month I have a full moon party for gringos and Panamanians. Usually, there are about sixty people, but it might be smaller this month because some are on vacation," our host told us as she showed us around. We quickly learned everyone in the one-bus-stop town knew her.

Breese made a birthday cake for two of our host's friends. The guys strung rope to keep little ones off the red dirt from a pool construction project. Chris sprayed down the tile porch and prepared for her friends. We moved chairs, set up tables, fluffed pillows, swept leaves, and then went kayaking in the sea, waiting for guests to arrive.

Conversations were in Spanish and English. There were chips and dip, ring toss, and lightning bugs, and several countries represented. When the party was in full force, and the band played a soundtrack for dancing, I stepped away to take the view from a distance. It was bittersweet. We spent the last weekend of our travels helping throw a party to bridge cultures. I couldn't have planned a better end.

Minds Set on Home

There was no way to resist how our thoughts turned toward home. It was strange to realize life moved on while we were gone. In that parallel universe, seniors we loved graduated. We sat on screens connected to Facebook Live to watch their big moments unfold. I was salsa dancing under buntings in Colombia instead of helping hang graduation banners at home. My niece went from talking in short phrases to complete sentences. Our next-door neighbors welcomed their first baby, and other dear friends welcomed their son. Favorite businesses closed and others opened. Driver's licenses were gained. Illnesses, new jobs, and loss marked the months we missed. Our

roots were lovingly and intentionally planted in a small plot of Oklahoma soil, but we would not return to life as before. In each place we stood, we left some of ourselves behind and picked up something to take home. Soon, we'd discover what grew and faded away while we were gone.

The year had been our once-in-a-lifetime opportunity, and we had seized it wholeheartedly. Living out of backpacks and traveling as a family of seven took work, but it never truly felt like it. My kids weren't perfect, and neither were their parents, but they dealt with being uncomfortable, tired, hungry, and so much more with humor, grace, and a perspective of adventure. They learned to look at the unknown not through a lens of fear but as an invitation to something new. They were my dream travel partners.

I recognized that the seven of us would never again spend an entire year trekking the globe together. My kids had adventures to chase, and I would figure out what life looked like for me after our big dream. I was sure we'd stand at borders and get passport stamps together again, but I was also confident we would never do *this* again. It had been a time to see the world's wonder and recognize it daily in each other. The ample margin in our days allowed us to deepen our understanding of the globe and cultivate relationships within our family. Sibling bonds were strengthened while Chris and I had a season of feeling completely in sync. I was profoundly grateful for the opportunity and heartsick to see it end.

The ample margin in our days allowed us to deepen our understanding of the globe and cultivate relationships within our family.

Breese joined me for a tearful sunrise walk on the beach on our final morning. Like her mom, she deeply grieved the trip's ending. We didn't talk much and didn't need to. One foot in front of the other, all the way to the airport and into our seats. The pilot told us to prepare for landing. It was time to go home.

WISDOM AND WONDER

We wrapped up our trip discussing how we would answer "How was your trip?"—knowing most people would only want to hear "It was good." We came up with three-second, three-minute, and three-cups-of-coffee answers. I warned the kids, as much as myself, that most people would only want the three-second answer. And it was okay; we had each other. One of the greatest gifts of traveling as a family was having six others who would understand when a *tres leches* down the road reminded us of one from Albania or how a quinoa bowl transported us back to a beach in Indonesia. We would always have someone to reminisce with.

Cultural Insights

As with many cities we visited, the oldest areas of town taught lessons on gentrification. Walking the streets of the world was a crash course in seeing how the character of a community changed as residents and businesses with wealth moved in and often displaced those of lower income. The complicated issue marked towns worldwide, including my district in Oklahoma. The disparity that can happen a block over can be mind-boggling.

Travel Tip: End a Trip with Intention

As our family tried to put into words our respective and collective experiences, we found that having debriefing questions was of great value, help, and comfort. There were so many emotions and thoughts to sift through. These questions got us all talking, thinking, laughing, and beginning the beautiful process of gathering our own wisdom and wonder to carry into the rest of our life journeys:

- If we did the whole trip over, what would you do differently?
- Do you have any new dreams or visions for your life that you didn't have before we left?
- What area of the trip did you struggle with the most?
- What was easy about a year of travel?
- What do you anticipate being the hardest about being home?
- What are you looking forward to in the future?
- What have you learned, and what will you do with it?
- Any regrets?
- What will you do with your first moments alone at home?
- What is something about the world that is different from what you expected?
- What have you learned about yourself?
- What areas of life do you want to grow in?
- How will you continue to foster relationships within our family?
- What does it feel like to be you right now?

Your Adventure

How do you make the most of your privileges for good purposes when at home and when out in the world?

CHRIS

As soon as I could walk, adventure was on my mind. It didn't matter if someone else had been there before, because I hadn't. Getting a little taste of farm life as a child and Boy Scouts later down the road made me yearn for pioneer-like adventures. I vividly remember breaking safety rules because I loved the thrill of getting a little lost in the woods during games of capture the flag.

My older sister gave me my first opportunity to leave the country and realize that the world was full of awe and wonder. She let a preteen tag along while she served in a medical clinic among the Huasteca in Mexico. I was hooked, from the beauty of the land and people to the frequent *raspados* at the local market. In travel, I found something that made me come alive.

If I'm not careful, I can get caught up in daily bills and responsibilities and miss fully breathing in life in the way I think it was meant to be lived. When Ashley and I started talking about our yearlong adventure, I didn't fully appreciate what a gift it would be to share the common experience as a family. I can't believe what I would have missed out on if I outsourced the opportunity to experience the world with my kids to anyone else.

I saw their faces as they tasted a *roti* for the first time at the Chiang Mai night market.

I danced with them around a campfire in the Sahara Desert. I explored the depths of the Red Sea with my sons. Together, we made life-long memories we could look back on and say, "Remember when?" I wanted a family experience so ingrained that it couldn't be forgotten, and I am grateful that my kids wanted it with us too!

I might be one of the last generations to know life before technology put the world in my hands. I remember traveling in the back-country of China with paper maps and coins for calls and asking for travel tips from other travelers. The exaggerated stories from other backpackers were the go-to source for tips and itinerary ideas. However, legitimate obstacles kept people from roads less traveled. The world is more accessible and connected than at any time in history, and despite what the click-bait might say, we have less to be afraid of and more to explore than ever before.

Our year away gave me a chance to give my kids a taste of the globe and welcome them to an abundant buffet. The open road in the unfamiliar was the perfect playground for us to figure things out together, gaining insight into each other and the world.

HOME

Coming home felt bittersweet to each of us. We decided to give family and friends a fake return date. The extroverts were excited to surprise others, and the introverts needed a few hours of sleep to acclimate and ease back in before seeing others. The friends renting our house moved out and left a hidden key for us. We awkwardly entered through the side door. The emptiness of the rooms and the bare walls magnified the size. Exhausted, we crashed. We surprised our family and friends early the following day by popping in unexpectedly at random places. Our first two days back overflowed with the goodness of reconnecting.

On our third night home, I settled in on the back porch to the gentle patter of summer rain and remembered the decade I spent in the same outdoor chair, questioning the likelihood of our trip. I reflected on the days before we bought our home when I perched on the back steps and imagined raising a family beneath the giant sycamore tree that towered over the yard.

I sipped on sparkling water—a brand from Italy my mom and a friend knew I liked, so they tracked some down as a welcome-home gift. Hudson was forty-five minutes away at the lake with friends. Everett was out of state, surprising teammates at a basketball tournament. Evann was knee-deep in Legos with the neighbors, Corbett was asleep, and Chris was in his office. Breese and I were in tears again. An empty backpack was open on the floor of my room. A year of travel took about four minutes to unpack physically. I'd be unpacking it in other ways for the rest of my life.

> A year of travel took about four minutes to unpack physically. I'd be unpacking it in other ways for the rest of my life.

The profound sadness that our days of wandering were over, that my kids were in different places, felt like a heavy cloud over me. It felt messy, and I felt lost. I was home, but it wasn't the one I left. I had never been here before. I understood reverse culture shock and how to walk through it, but the cause of this ache was something different. It was living fully awake and alive in a dream I had doubted was possible and then grappling with its end. It was experiencing the overwhelming wonder of the world and its people and the excitement they brought each day. It was also the reality of the parenting season I was entering. Corbett was nineteen. Hudson would soon begin his senior year. Everett would be driving, and my youngest would become a teenager. My chicks would leave the nest, and the whole world would now have a wide-open door of possibility. Seasons were changing, and I was a fan of perpetual summer.

Our First Week Home

We unpacked boxes with our dishes, our bedding, and my ridiculous number of throw pillows. My dad delivered a countertop *shawarma* machine for Everett, who requested to roast meat 24/7. He also grew twenty bougainvillea in little pots for me in our absence. Granted, my parents have never sown thoughtfulness sparingly, but I was deeply moved by their gifts of generosity and significance. Bougainvillea swayed in the wind, climbed arched doorways, and greeted me in every country. Its spread around the world was linked to Jeanne Baret, the first woman believed to have circumnavigated the globe. I developed a deep fondness for its hardiness, vibrant colors, and ability to grow in any warm condition.

Friends anticipated my difficult reentry and lovingly planted mint in a small flower bed in my yard so we could make Moroccan tea. I smiled as I watered my new plants, tangible signs of those close by who love us so well and of the new friends made and known only briefly on the journey.

During our reflection time in Panama, we shared regrets about our trip. My only remorse was not buying the striped rug in Mostar, Bosnia and Herzegovina. Chris pulled out a yellow package with *Sarajevo* written on the sides. I cut open the tape to discover the rug. Walking past it ten months before, I admired it but never said anything to Chris, reminding myself that we weren't shopping on our trip—and knowing he'd buy it if I made a big deal about it. He snuck away from our Airbnb one night, bought it, and shipped it home. It was a risky bet on his part, but such a good one. Of all the incredible handiwork I saw on our travels, the one item I regretted not buying was now in my living room. It hangs on a wall as a picture of a remarkable year we fought for together, but even more as a reflection of how Chris is always looking for ways to make me smile.

I begrudgingly bought a calendar. For a year, we only had to know the day or month if there was a plane to catch. Life was slow, restful, simple. A calendar meant a return to schedules and commitments. Traveling had been a lengthy exhale, a yearlong

Sabbath. But exhales must become inhales, and Sabbaths are meant to be a pause, not a permanent state.

Preserving a Traveler's Mind

We returned to the grocery store, library, and Everett's summer basketball league. Evann got the kitten she had waited years for and named her Ali in honor of her favorite country, Albania. Teenagers and chocolate chip cookies filled my kitchen again. We resumed our weekly donut date with my grandma and extended family. Nearly a decade earlier, my grandparents began a Thursday morning donut tradition to spend more time with all of us, and it stuck. We likely developed a fondness for all those sticky tables around the world after gathering every week for chocolate long johns and glazed donut holes. While we were gone, new owners took over "our" shop. A year away meant a clean break from routines and a chance to start over. Donut shops, like churches, are found every half a mile in my town. Instead of returning to our old shop, we opted to try something new. Our skill of flexibility was honed and ready to be used.

A friendly smile and a comforting accent welcomed me as I walked through the door of the shop closest to our house. It felt strangely familiar. English spoken with an accent unlike mine had been my daily soundtrack for months, and it was good to hear it again. I placed my order and looked around to find a way to connect. In the corner hung a calendar with Korean Hangul letters. Perfect.

"Thank you," I said, smiling as she rang up my order. "What is that picture of on your calendar?" I asked.

She looked up and grinned. "It's a Korean church."

"I'd love to visit Korea one day! I recently visited Southeast Asia and already miss it," I responded as another customer walked in, cutting our conversation short.

We found our new donut shop.

My girls and I joined their cousins for manicures and pedicures. My father-in-law wanted to take all of his granddaughters out for the experience. I took my place in the row of seats. Before long, I learned the woman helping me was from Vietnam. I excitedly told her about my time there and listed my favorite foods: *pho, cao lau, chao, bun cha,* and *banh mi.* I asked her what she missed about Vietnam and shared how much I treasured my time there. Before I left, I asked her for restaurant recommendations, and we exchanged numbers. I was determined to seek out the global, locally.

A Wider Lens for New Choices

Hudson and Everett joined friends for camp—they 100 percent packed more stuff for five days than they did for a year. Jokingly, I told them not to cry themselves to sleep at night missing me, as I knew it would be so hard after being together 24/7 for a year. Everett packed items from South America for the "America" theme night. I loved seeing how my kids' worldviews had expanded due to international travel. I know the theme was probably intended to be "United States of America," but I liked that leaving off the "United States" part opened the door for him to creatively celebrate a fuller view of all the Americas he loved.

We all felt a little lost in the familiar. The more we reconnected with others, the more I heard, "I bet you're so glad to be home!" The expected response would have been "Yes! It's so good to be back!" And while it was true, it also wasn't. Instead, I leaned into the awkward, but truthful response: "Not really. The last year was beyond my wildest dreams. I miss it." Cue the confused facial responses. I wasn't sure how to talk about what I experienced, and others seemed unsure how to ask. The kids repeatedly heard from friends, "It's like you didn't even leave," which was hard to hear when they felt their entire world had changed. We had been right; most only wanted the three-second answer, which was more than okay and completely understandable. The seven of us reminisced, laughed, and struggled through the complexity together.

Each day over the following weeks and months, I saw the influence of our trip play out in different ways. My kids came home from events, parties, and coffee shops with stories of people they met from other countries. Familiar with being the outsiders, the ones who didn't know the language, culture, or details obvious to everyone else, they grew eyes for kindred spirits visiting our country. They knew what it was like to stand out as a visitor and be welcomed with unflinching kindness, and they wanted to do the same for others. Proactively seeking out international grocery stores, restaurants, and events that celebrated other cultures, they consistently made connections between home and the places they traveled.

Breese whipped up *khao soi* as a comfort meal for me on days I missed travel a little extra. Enrolling her in a cooking class in Thailand was one of the more brilliant moves I made on the trip. Evann continued trying new foods and embracing uncomfortable situations. On the first cold day of fall, all three boys came downstairs wearing their alpaca sweaters from Ecuador. I laughed at the sight of their unplanned matchy-matchiness.

There were a handful of activities and routines we knew with certainty we'd be coming home to. Everett playing basketball was possibly the most certain thing of our return. He played hundreds of games worldwide and looked forward to returning to his team. Basketball was a given. And then, all of a sudden, it wasn't. Plot twists as we traveled never surprised me. Pivots at home came far more shockingly. He deeply loved the game and loved his friends, but there were other areas in which he wanted to

experience growth and more things he wanted to pursue. High school sports schedules don't leave a lot of wiggle room. It was a huge decision that meant not being a part of the team, which affected nearly every area of his life, especially friendships. I was so proud of him for thinking through what he wanted and making a tough call.

Our kids gained a different perspective on how they used their time, what equaled a fulfilling life, and the reality that their days were numbered. We watched them make thoughtful and brave decisions and change course on many paths we once thought were cemented. Everett joined our city's youth council and a youth program with the police. Corbett became the youngest Rotarian in our town. They traveled to see a large-scale perspective of the world, then plugged back in their small community with renewed vision and purpose. I began to learn when one of my kids said, "Hey, Mom, I've been thinking..." I should expect the unexpected. Of course, other times, I wondered if they remembered the trip at all. At night, I'd walk into the kitchen to find seventeen glasses and eight dish towels left on the counter. I would then question how we had ever survived a year with only one water bottle each. For the love of your mother, please use only one glass!

Relearning Home

The hardest part of international travel for me remained the sense of isolation I felt once at home. I struggled at basketball games when adults yelled at players, coaches, and referees, missing the camaraderie I witnessed on public courts worldwide where more joy and less animosity filled the bleachers. I wrestled with what to say when I heard unwarranted safety assumptions about places I loved from people who had never set foot in those communities. The headlines fed fear, and as with fast food, consumption required no work. I found myself cringing at false narratives about faiths spoken by those who didn't even know someone practicing the faith. I felt all tangled up inside, caught in a sacred wrestling match.

Leaving for our trip meant ending commitments I had held for years, some nearly two decades. As we traveled, I watched from afar how things continued perfectly fine without me. It was eye-opening and freeing to see how replaceable I was. I wasn't needed, which released me from the sense of obligation but was also confusing. I had to figure out what things had run their course and what things I wanted to return to. I sat at familiar tables with familiar faces, feeling entirely out of place. How do I step back into a life that no longer seems to fit?

The kids wrestled with some of the same things. We stopped some activities and commitments, and we started others. Our days were far slower than before we left, and the lingering we did around little tables across the world turned into lounging together in our kitchen. Travels tethered us in a new way, and I rested in it. Breese took over placing our donut orders each week. She practiced Korean as she built bridges over sausage rolls and fried dough. We became regulars at local international markets and attempted to re-create our favorite cultural dishes. Everett learned to make *pupusas*, Hudson introduced his friends to Moroccan tea, and Corbett discovered new food trucks. Evann continued to put her water bottle in the fridge, a habit she picked up traveling when there was no ice. I hung colorful tile and big floral wallpaper in my kitchen, reminders of the vibrant places we visited. I stayed up to date with the library calendar, circling international festivals and events. We continued to learn from the world within a few miles of our home. Sunset views from our front porch astonished us as we closed out days with neighbors and went inside to watch the most recent K-drama. Our home became a cultural melting pot simmering with the best of home and abroad.

Where to Next?

Six months after our return, we boarded a plane to Central America for ten days. Instead of celebrating Christmas with gifts, we kept an eye on tickets to anywhere new and warm at any time and found an incredibly cheap option to Guatemala. The best deal meant driving five hours to Dallas and flying with only a small "personal item" bag each (no carry-ons, no checked bags), which was easy for ten days after a year of backpack living. It immediately felt like we had never stopped traveling. We all fell seamlessly into our old vagabond routines. The guys poked fun at my common travel phrase "Times that by seven," which was my go-to response for everything from bus tickets to soft-serve ice cream. There was also "You don't know how that translates," which I used each time Hudson tried to shadowbox me or mess with his sister in front of others, not knowing how his actions could be perceived in various cultures. Exploring Guatemala put the wind back in my sails and reminded me I could have roots and wings. Everett began dreaming up an accommodation empire—owning places worldwide for travelers of different budgets. Breese made plans to return to Antigua to live for a year one day. Hudson talked about moving to a Spanish-speaking country for immersive language learning. Corbett closed a real estate deal while sitting at a taco shop. Evann missed her cat.

Life would keep changing, but I had a good feeling that for as long as possible we'd figure out ways to travel together. I wanted to see as much of the world as possible because someone I love created it. In the meantime, I'd figure out how to be awestruck by a place I knew like the back of my hand. I'd keep my eyes open and let it surprise me like the world did. Curiosity had been my favorite tour guide. It led us to all the places we remembered most, and I looked to it to guide me at home.

Where do I want to go next?

Anywhere I've never been.

NOTES

Unlike many travel books, this is not a guide. Out of respect, I have purposefully chosen to omit the names of small towns. My hope is that by sharing our stories, readers won't walk away with a list of places to check off but will feel empowered and inspired to dive into local communities and discover the beauty every corner holds.

Slovenia and Croatia
Dunking Devils Squad. "Chose Your Character." Instagram, September 20, 2022. www.instagram.com/reel/CivGmrhpyGa/.

Albania
Solomon, Marty, and Brent Billings, hosts. "Kate Schmidgall—BitterSweet." *BEMA Podcast.* April 21, 2022. https://www.bemadiscipleship.com/275.

Vietnam
Anthony Bourdain, "Bourdain falls in love with Vietnam's street food (Parts Unknown)," uploaded by CNN, October 12, 2014, YouTube video, 0:19, https://www.youtube.com/watch?v=NMrgQ_dOyhk.

Ecuador
Compassion International. "What Is the Opposite of Poverty?" Children and Poverty. www.compassion.com/poverty/opposite-of-poverty.htm.

ACKNOWLEDGMENTS

The original manuscript for this book was written during the first six months after our return home as a way for me to process our year. It began as a record of our adventures for my future grandkids in the hope that they would experience the beauty of the world through the stories of their grandparents, parents, aunts, and uncles.

To those worldwide who welcomed us into their homes, communities, and basketball courts, your kindness, hospitality, and generosity shaped our view of the world as a place full of hope, deep goodness, and ridiculously delicious food. I hope the stories in this book honor you and give readers a glimpse into the beauty beyond the borders they've known.

To Cindy, Christy, and Amy, thank you for reading the early chapters of this book—the ones written before there was a publishing contract. You kept asking for more, and your excitement (even when I asked for critiques) put wind in my sails to keep going.

To our family and friends, you've cheered us on, read pages of edited stories, texted to check in on me throughout the process, and supported us in immeasurable ways—thank you. I am wildly excited to experience as much of the world as I can, but the slice of it I call mine will always be the one I get to share with you.

To the Under the Sycamore community, you have encouraged me for nearly two decades. This book went from a personal project to a published reality because you told me others would find its message valuable. Thank you for traveling with us and making the online world beautiful.

To Liz Burns, Anne Hammond, and Brenda Lewis, teachers are influential voices. You were the first ones to call me a writer. Your words play in my mind each time I pick up a pen or tap a keyboard. Thank you.

To Haverlee, thank you for poring over every chapter and providing insightful perspectives. I am indebted to you.

To Paul Nielsen and Jeff Miller of Faceout Studio, and Nicole Dougherty and the Harvest House team, thank you for listening to my voice both in the design process and in the words written. I imagined a beautiful book reflecting a vibrant world, and you brought it to life.

To Hope Lyda, I could not have dreamed of working with a more perfect editor. Thank you for helping me fine-tune the words, providing structure, and offering the critical feedback I needed. Your lovely handprints are all over these pages.

To Heather Green of Harvest House, this book directly results from your confidence in me and your personal support to make it happen. I knew I had someone in my corner from the very start. Thank you for taking a risk on me and believing it would be worth it.

To Lesley, thank you for supporting us as we chase adventure and for creating the lovely bougainvillea art. I cherish having your talent included in these pages. I love you.

To Corbett, thank you for sharing your camera as we traveled and for allowing me to use some of your photos throughout these pages. For the record, I took the one on page 38.

To Mom and Dad, traveling the world felt like "no big deal" because I learned from you that pretty much everything in life can be figured out. Thank you for supporting our dreams even when it meant a difficult year for you. You are thoughtful and generous and are always up for helping me with any project. I love you.

To Corbett, Hudson, Everett, Breese, and Evann, I'll linger with you around sticky plastic tables anywhere. You know firsthand how the world overflows with places to explore and celebrate. I hope all your journeys include a bit of meandering and wonder! I'll cheer you on as you chase your own adventures and will always respond with an emphatic "Absolutely!" to any invitations you extend my way. Thank you for trusting me and supporting me as I shared our stories. You are my favorite and the delight of my life. I love you.

To Chris, we actually did it! Thank you for choosing a path that included years of sacrifice and intentional decisions to chase after our dream. Goodness, it was worth it. Your excitement for life, unabashed joy in meeting people, and thrill for exploring the unknown are contagious. Thank you for all the passenger-seat conversations you endured so I could bounce in the back of pickup trucks. You love me and our kids so well. I love you.

To my heavenly Father, thank you for the ways you reveal yourself to us through the people and places you've created. It truly is a spectacular world!

ABOUT THE AUTHOR

Ashley Campbell is not a *New York Times* bestselling author. She has never edited a magazine, worked in the travel industry, or acquired accolades that deem her a writer. Nonetheless, storytelling and photography are her favorite mediums for celebrating the beauty of life. She updates the paint on her walls more than the clothes in her closet and is a living oxymoron of intentionally growing her roots for four decades in the same town while daily checking for flight deals to somewhere new. Her five kids affectionately poke fun at her most-used travel phrases: "I don't know—I've never been here before," "We can walk," and "Times that by seven." Their home in Oklahoma revolves around the ideas that building tables is better than building fences, cookies should be shared, and adding more color is always good.

@underthesycamore

ashleyannphotography.com